CATCH-22

Joseph Heller

This edition published by Spark Publishing

Spark Publishing
A Division of SparkNotes LLC
120 Fifth Avenue, 8th Floor
New York, NY 10011

Please submit all comments and questions or report errors to www.sparknotes.com/errors

Printed and bound in the United States

ISBN 1-58663-381-3

Contents

CONTEXT

J OSEPH HELLER WAS BORN in Brooklyn in 1923. He served as an Air Force bombardier in World War II and enjoyed a long career as a writer and a teacher. His best-selling books include *Something Happened, Good as Gold, Picture This, God Knows,* and *Closing Time,* but his first novel, *Catch-22,* remains his most famous and acclaimed work. He died of a heart attack in December 1999.

Heller wrote *Catch-22* while working at a New York City marketing firm producing ad copy. The novel draws heavily on his Air Force experience and presents a war story that is at once hilarious, grotesque, cynical, and stirring. The novel generated a great deal of controversy upon its initial publication in 1961. Critics tended either to adore it or despise it, and those who hated it did so for the same reasons as the critics who loved it. Over time, *Catch-22* has become one of the defining novels of the twentieth century. It presents an utterly unsentimental vision of war, stripping all romantic pretenses away from combat, replacing visions of glory and honor with a kind of nightmarish comedy of violence, bureaucracy, and paradoxical madness. This kind of irony has come to be expected of war novels since the Vietnam War, but in the wake of World War II, which most Americans believed was a just and heroic war, *Catch-22* was shocking. It proved almost prophetic about both the Vietnam War, a conflict that began a few years after the novel was originally published, and the sense of disillusionment about the military that many Americans experienced during this conflict.

Unlike other antiromantic war novels, such as Erich Maria Remarque's *All Quiet on the Western Front, Catch-22* relies heavily on humor to convey the insanity of war, presenting the horrible meaninglessness of armed conflict through a kind of desperate absurdity rather than through graphic depictions of suffering and violence. *Catch-22* also distinguishes itself from other antiromantic war novels through its core values: the story of Yossarian, the protagonist, is ultimately not one of despair but one of hope. He believes that the positive urge to live and to be free can redeem the individual from the dehumanizing machinery of war. The novel is told as a series of loosely related, tangential stories in no particular chronological order. The narrative that emerges from this structural

1

tangle upholds the value of the individual in the face of the impersonal, collective military mass; at every stage it mocks insincerity and hypocrisy, even when such values appear triumphant.

Despite its World War II setting, *Catch-22* is often thought of as a signature novel of the 1960s and 1970s. It was during those decades that American youth truly began to question authority. Hippies, university protests, and the civil rights movement all marked the 1960s as a decade of revolution, and Heller's novel fit in perfectly with the spirit of the times. In fact, Heller once said, "I wasn't interested in the war in *Catch-22*. I was interested in the personal relationships in bureaucratic authority." Whether Heller was using the war to comment on authority or using bureaucracy as a statement about the war, it is clear that *Catch-22* is more than just a war novel. It is also a novel about the moral choices that every person must make when faced with a system of authority whose rules are both immoral and illogical.

PLOT OVERVIEW

DURING THE SECOND HALF of World War II, a soldier named Yossarian is stationed with his Air Force squadron on the island of Pianosa, near the Italian coast in the Mediterranean Sea. Yossarian and his friends endure a nightmarish, absurd existence defined by bureaucracy and violence: they are inhuman resources in the eyes of their blindly ambitious superior officers. The squadron is thrown thoughtlessly into brutal combat situations and bombing runs in which it is more important for the squadron members to capture good aerial photographs of explosions than to destroy their targets. Their colonels continually raise the number of missions that they are required to fly before being sent home, so that no one is ever sent home. Still, no one but Yossarian seems to realize that there is a war going on; everyone thinks he is crazy when he insists that millions of people are trying to kill him.

Yossarian's story forms the core of the novel, so most events are refracted through his point of view. Yossarian takes the whole war personally: unswayed by national ideals or abstract principles, Yossarian is furious that his life is in constant danger through no fault of his own. He has a strong desire to live and is determined to be immortal or die trying. As a result, he spends a great deal of his time in the hospital, faking various illnesses in order to avoid the war. As the novel progresses through its loosely connected series of recurring stories and anecdotes, Yossarian is continually troubled by his memory of Snowden, a soldier who died in his arms on a mission when Yossarian lost all desire to participate in the war. Yossarian is placed in ridiculous, absurd, desperate, and tragic circumstances—he sees friends die and disappear, his squadron get bombed by its own mess officer, and colonels and generals volunteer their men for the most perilous battle in order to enhance their own reputations.

Catch-22 is a law defined in various ways throughout the novel. First, Yossarian discovers that it is possible to be discharged from military service because of insanity. Always looking for a way out, Yossarian claims that he is insane, only to find out that by claiming that he is insane he has proved that he is obviously sane—since any sane person would claim that he or she is insane in order to avoid flying bombing missions. Elsewhere, Catch-22 is defined as a law that is illegal to read. Ironically, the place where it is written that it is illegal is in Catch-22 itself. It is yet again defined as the law that the enemy is allowed to do anything that one can't keep him from doing. In short, then, Catch-22 is any paradoxical, circular reasoning that catches its victim in its illogic and serves those who have made the law. Catch-22 can be found in the novel not only where it is explicitly defined but also throughout the characters' stories, which are full of catches and instances of circular reasoning that trap unwitting bystanders in their snares—for instance, the ability of the powerful officer Milo Minderbinder to make great sums of money by trading among the companies that he himself owns.

As Yossarian struggles to stay alive, a number of secondary stories unfold around him. His friend Nately falls in love with a whore from Rome and woos her constantly, despite her continued indifference and the fact that her kid sister constantly interferes with their romantic rendezvous. Finally, she falls in love with Nately, but he is killed on his very next mission. When Yossarian brings her the bad news, she blames him for Nately's death and tries to stab him every time she sees him thereafter. Another subplot follows the rise of the black-market empire of Milo Minderbinder, the squadron's mess hall officer. Milo runs a syndicate in which he borrows military planes and pilots to transport food between various points in Europe, making a massive profit from his sales. Although he claims that "everyone has a share" in the syndicate, this promise is later proven false. Milo's enterprise flourishes nonetheless, and he is revered almost religiously by communities all over Europe.

The novel draws to a close as Yossarian, troubled by Nately's death, refuses to fly any more missions. He wanders the streets of Rome, encountering every kind of human horror—rape, disease, murder. He is eventually arrested for being in Rome without a pass, and his superior officers, Colonel Cathcart and Colonel Korn, offer him a choice. He can either face a court-martial or be released and sent home with an honorable discharge. There is only one condition: in order to be released, he must approve of Cathcart and Korn and state his support for their policy, which requires all the men in the squadron to fly eighty missions. Although he is tempted by the offer, Yossarian realizes that to comply would be to endanger the lives of other innocent men. He chooses another way out, deciding to desert the army and flee to neutral Sweden. In doing so, he turns his back on the dehumanizing machinery of the military, rejects the rule of Catch-22, and strives to gain control of his own life.

CHARACTER LIST

Yossarian   The protagonist and hero of the novel. Yossarian is a captain in the Air Force and a lead bombardier in his squadron, but he hates the war. His powerful desire to live has led him to the conclusion that millions of people are trying to kill him, and he has decided either to live forever or, ironically, die trying.

Milo Minderbinder   A fantastically powerful mess officer, Milo controls an international black-market syndicate and is revered in obscure corners all over the world. He ruthlessly chases after profit and bombs his own men as part of a contract with Germany. Milo insists that everyone in the squadron will benefit from being part of the syndicate and that "everyone has a share." He also takes his job as mess officer very, very seriously; as a result, the troops in Yossarian's division eat better than any others.

Doc Daneeka   The medical officer. Doc Daneeka feels very sorry for himself because the war has interrupted his lucrative private practice in the United States, and he refuses to listen to other people's problems. Doc Daneeka is the first person to explain Catch-22 to Yossarian.

The chaplain   A friend of Yossarian. Timid and thoughtful, the chaplain is haunted by a sensation of déjà vu (the feeling of having seen or experienced a particular thing before) and begins to lose his faith in God as the novel progresses.

Colonel Cathcart The ambitious, unintelligent officer in charge of Yossarian's squadron. Colonel Cathcart wants to be a general, and he tries to impress his superiors by bravely volunteering his men for dangerous combat duty whenever he gets the chance. As he tries to scheme his way ahead, he considers successful actions "feathers in his cap" and unsuccessful ones "black eyes."

Hungry Joe An unhinged member of Yossarian's squadron. A former photographer for *Life* magazine, Hungry Joe is obsessed with photographing naked women. He has horrible nightmares on nights when he is *not* scheduled to fly a combat mission the next morning.

Nately A good-natured nineteen-year-old boy in Yossarian's squadron. Nately, who comes from a wealthy home, falls in love with a whore in Rome and generally tries to keep Yossarian from getting into trouble.

Nately's whore The beautiful whore with whom Nately falls in love in Rome.

McWatt A cheerful, polite pilot who often flies Yossarian's planes. McWatt likes to joke around with Yossarian and sometimes buzzes the squadron.

Clevinger An idealistic member of Yossarian's squadron. Clevinger firmly believes in such concepts as country, loyalty, and duty, and argues about them with Yossarian.

Dobbs A co-pilot, Dobbs seizes the controls from Huple during the mission to Avignon, the same mission on which Snowden died.

Dunbar A friend of Yossarian and the only other person who seems to understand that there is a war going on. Dunbar has decided to live as long as possible by making time pass as slowly as possible, so he treasures boredom and discomfort.

Major Major Major Major The supremely mediocre squadron commander. Born Major Major Major, he is promoted to major on his first day in the army by a mischievous computer. Major Major is painfully awkward and will see people in his office only when he is not there. His promotion to squadron commander distances him from the other soldiers, reducing him to loneliness.

Major — — de Coverley The fierce, intense executive officer of the squadron. Major —— de Coverley is revered and feared by the men. They are afraid to ask his first name, even though all he does is play horseshoes and rent apartments for the officers in cities taken by American forces.

Aarfy Yossarian's navigator, even though he gets lost wherever he goes. Aarfy infuriates Yossarian by pretending that he cannot hear Yossarian's orders during bombing runs.

Orr Yossarian's often-maddening roommate. Orr is a gifted fix-it man who is always constructing little improvements to the tent that he shares with Yossarian. He almost always crashes his plane or is shot down on combat missions, but he always manages to survive.

Appleby A handsome, athletic member of the squadron and a superhuman Ping-Pong player. Orr enigmatically says that Appleby has flies in his eyes.

Captain Black The squadron's bitter intelligence officer. Captain Black wants nothing more than to be squadron commander. He exults in the men's discomfort and does everything he can to increase it; when Nately falls in love with a whore in Rome, Captain Black begins to buy her services regularly just to taunt him.

Lieutenant Colonel Korn Colonel Cathcart's wily, cynical sidekick.

Major Danby The timid operations officer. Before the war, Danby was a college professor; now, he does his best for his country.

General Dreedle A grumpy old general in charge of the wing in which Yossarian's squadron is placed. General Dreedle is the victim of a private war waged against him by the ambitious General Peckem.

Nurse Duckett A nurse in the Pianosa hospital who becomes Yossarian's lover.

Chief White Halfoat An alcoholic Native American from Oklahoma who has decided to die of pneumonia.

Havermeyer A fearless lead bombardier. Havermeyer never takes evasive action, and he enjoys shooting field mice at night.

Huple A fifteen-year-old pilot who was flying the mission to Avignon on which Snowden was killed. Huple is Hungry Joe's roommate; his cat likes to sleep on Hungry Joe's face.

Washington Irving A famous American author whose name Yossarian signs to letters during one of his many stays in the hospital. Eventually, military intelligence believes Washington Irving to be the name of a covert insubordinate, and two C.I.D. (Criminal Investigation Division) men are dispatched to ferret him out of the squadron.

Luciana A beautiful girl Yossarian meets, sleeps with, and falls in love with during a brief period in Rome.

Mudd Generally referred to as "the dead man in Yossarian's tent," Mudd was a squadron member who was killed in action before he could be processed as an official member of the squadron. As a result, he is listed as never having arrived, and no one has the authority to move his belongings out of Yossarian's tent.

Lieutenant Scheisskopf Later a colonel and eventually a general. Scheisskopf, whose name is German for "shithead," helps train Yossarian's squadron in America and shows an unsettling passion for elaborate military parades.

The soldier in white A body completely covered with bandages in Yossarian and Dunbar's ward in the Pianosa hospital. The body terrifies the men.

Snowden The young gunner whose death over Avignon shattered Yossarian's courage and caused him to experience the shock of war. Snowden died in Yossarian's arms with his entrails splattered all over Yossarian's uniform, a trauma that is gradually revealed over the course of the novel.

Corporal Whitcomb The chaplain's atheist assistant, and later a sergeant. Corporal Whitcomb hates the chaplain for holding back his career and makes the chaplain a suspect in the Washington Irving scandal.

Ex-p.f.c. Wintergreen The mail clerk at the Twenty-seventh Air Force Headquarters, Wintergreen is able to intercept and forge documents and thus wields enormous power in the Air Force. He continually goes AWOL (Absent Without Leave) and is continually punished with loss of rank.

General Peckem The ambitious special operations general who plots incessantly to take over General Dreedle's position.

Kid Sampson A pilot in the squadron.

Colonel Moodus General Dreedle's son-in-law. General Dreedle despises Colonel Moodus and enjoys watching Chief White Halfoat bust him in the nose.

Flume Chief White Halfoat's old roommate, who is so afraid of having his throat slit while he sleeps that he has taken to living in the forest.

Lieutenant Scheisskopf's wife The lieutenant's wife and the lover of all the men in her husband's squadron, including Yossarian, with whom she debates about God.

Analysis of Major Characters

Yossarian

John Yossarian, the protagonist of *Catch-22,* is both a member of the squadron's community and alienated by it. Although he flies and lives with the men, he is marked as an outsider by the fact that many of the men think he is insane. Even his Assyrian name is unusual; no one has ever heard it before. His difference from the rest of the men leads us to expect something exceptional from Yossarian.

But Yossarian's characteristics are not those of a typical hero. He does not risk his life to save others; in fact, his primary goal throughout the novel is to *avoid* risking his life whenever possible. But the system of values around Yossarian is so skewed that this approach seems to be the only truly moral stance he can take, if only because it is so logical. What we come to hate about military bureaucracy as we read *Catch-22* is its lack of logic; men are asked to risk their lives again and again for reasons that are utterly illogical and unimportant. In this illogical world, Yossarian seizes hold of one true, logical idea—that he should try to preserve life. Unlike a conventional hero, however, Yossarian does not generalize this idea to mean that he should risk his own life in attempts to save everybody else's. In a world where life itself is so undervalued and so casually lost, it is possible to redefine heroism as simple self-preservation.

This insistence on self-preservation creates a conflict for Yossarian. Even though he is determined to save his own life at all costs, he nonetheless cares deeply for the other members of his squadron and is traumatized by their deaths. His ongoing horror at Snowden's death stems both from his pity for Snowden and from his horrified realization that his own body is just as destructible as Snowden's. In the end, when offered a choice between his own safety and the safety of the entire squadron, Yossarian is unable to choose himself over others. This concern for others complicates the simple logic of self-preservation, and creates its own Catch-22: life is not worth living without a moral concern for the well-being of others, but a moral concern for the well-being of others endangers one's life. Yossarian ultimately escapes this conundrum by literally walking away from the war—an action that refuses both the possibility of becoming an officer who avoids danger at the expense of his troops and that of remaining a soldier who risks his life for meaningless reasons.

MILO MINDERBINDER

Representing an extreme version of capitalist free enterprise that has spiraled out of control, Milo seems simultaneously brilliant and insane. What starts out as a business in black-market eggs turns into a worldwide enterprise in which, he claims, "everyone has a share." At first, Milo's syndicate seems like a bit of harmless profiteering; we cheer for Milo because he is at least making money at the expense of the ridiculous bureaucracy that perpetuates the war. Like Yossarian, he bends the rules toward his own benefit; his quest for profit seems logical compared to the way Colonel Cathcart sends his men to their deaths just so he can get a promotion. All the men seem to like Milo, and they are perfectly willing to fly him to places like Malta and Egypt so that he can buy and sell his goods.

Milo's racket takes on a sinister air, however, when he bombs his own squadron as part of a deal he has made with the Germans. Many men are wounded or killed in this incident, and Milo's syndicate suddenly seems like an evil force that has expanded beyond anyone's ability to control it. But Milo's reasons for bombing the squadron are no more arbitrary than Colonel Cathcart's ambitiously volunteering to send his men to dangerous Bologna. In fact, one could argue that Milo's actions are *more* rational than Cathcart's, since Milo is guaranteed a profit, whereas Cathcart does not really have a chance of becoming a general.

In many ways, Milo's character shows how capitalism transcends political ideology. We are never given any idea of what the war is being fought over, and the men have no sense of defending the ideals of their home country. Milo's ability to make money off of both friend and enemy, and his willingness to support whichever is more profitable, take advantage of the complete lack of ideology in *Catch*-22. Furthermore, his willingness to allow his own camp to be bombed shows his complete disregard for the sides drawn by the war, and the men's acceptance of payment for being bombed shows that Milo is not alone in placing a high value on making money.

THE CHAPLAIN

The horrors of war cause the chaplain to have his doubts about God, and he struggles to maintain his faith amid the senseless violence around him. One of the hardest things for the chaplain to deal with is the way that religion is constantly being co-opted for reasons having nothing to do with God or even with the comfort of the men. For example, the chaplain's atheistic assistant, Corporal Whitcomb, wants to send form letters home to the families of men killed and wounded in combat. The chaplain objects because the letters are insincere, but Colonel Cathcart insists on the form letters because he believes that they will bring him recognition. Such events force the chaplain to realize that religion is not valued on its own terms, but only as a tool that the officers can use to further their own causes.

When three men drag the chaplain into an isolated cellar and accuse him of unspecified crimes, he realizes that, because they have the power to beat him to death, his innocence has become irrelevant. Shortly afterward, the chaplain fakes an ailment and checks into the hospital. He has realized that trying to exist within the rules is impossible; having justified sin to himself, he feels much better.

The chaplain's character reminds us of one more way in which war upsets moral and ethical codes. Just as Doc Daneeka is confused about the role of a doctor in a world where man's primary goal is to cause injury and death, the chaplain is disoriented by a world where killing has become a virtue.

THEMES, MOTIFS & SYMBOLS

THEMES

Themes are the fundamental and often universal ideas explored in a literary work.

THE ABSOLUTE POWER OF BUREAUCRACY

One of the most terrifying aspects of *Catch-22* is the fact that the lives and deaths of the men in Yossarian's squadron are governed not by their own decisions concerning dangerous risks but by the decisions of an impersonal, frightening bureaucracy. The men must risk their lives even when they know that their missions are useless, as when they are forced to keep flying combat missions late in the novel even after they learn that the Allies have essentially won the war. The bureaucrats are absolutely deaf to any attempts that the men make to reason with them logically; they defy logic at every turn. Major Major, for example, will see people in his office only when he is not there, and Doc Daneeka won't ground Yossarian for insanity because Yossarian's desire to be grounded reveals that he must be sane.

Several scenes of interrogation add to the bureaucracy's frustrating refusal to listen to reason. In one such scene, Scheisskopf interrogates Clevinger but will not let Clevinger state his innocence because he is too busy correcting Clevinger's way of speaking. In another such scene, the chaplain is taken into a cellar and accused of a crime, but the men interrogating him do not know what the crime is—they hope to find out by interrogating him. In these and other instances, Yossarian's companions learn that what they do and say has very little effect on what happens to them. All they can do is learn to navigate their way through the bureaucracy, using its illogical rules to their own advantage whenever possible.

LOSS OF RELIGIOUS FAITH

Even the chaplain begins to doubt his faith in God by the end of Catch-22. His disillusionment stems in part from Colonel Cathcart's constant attempts to use the outward manifestations of religion to further his own ambition. Heller's treatment of the subject of God is most focused in the Thanksgiving discussion between Yossarian and Scheisskopf's wife. Both are atheists: Mrs. Scheisskopf does not believe in a just and loving God, whereas the God in whom Yossarian does not believe is a bumbling fool. Yossarian points out that no truly good, omniscient God would have created phlegm and tooth decay, let alone human suffering. Yossarian has experienced so many terrible things that he cannot believe in a God who would create such a wide array of options when it comes to pain and death. But the loss of faith in God does not mean a world without morals for the characters. Instead, it means a world in which each man must make his own morals—as Yossarian does when he chooses to desert the army rather than betray his squadron.

THE IMPOTENCE OF LANGUAGE
In the first chapter of *Catch-22*, we see Yossarian randomly deleting words from the letters that he is required to censor while he is in the hospital. At first, this act seems terrible: the letters are the men's only way of communicating with loved ones at home, and Yossarian is destroying that line of communication. As we learn more about Yossarian's world, however, we see that the military bureaucracy has taken the communicative power out of language. As Snowden dies in the back of the plane, all that Yossarian can think of to say is "there, there," over and over. He knows his words have no power to comfort Snowden, but he does not know what else to do. Faced with the realities of death and the absurdity of its circumstances, language seems unable to communicate any sort of reassurance.

While language has no power to comfort in the novel, it does have the power to circumvent logic and trap the squadron in an inescapable prison of bureaucracy. Catch-22 itself is nothing but a bunch of words strung together to circumvent logic and keep Yossarian flying missions. Catch-22 even contains a clause that makes it illegal to read Catch-22, demonstrating how absolutely powerful the concept of Catch-22 is. Yossarian knows that since it is nothing but words, Catch-22 does not really exist, but within the framework of the bureaucratic military, he has no choice but to accept the illogical prison in which these words place him.

THE INEVITABILITY OF DEATH
Yossarian's one goal—to stay alive or die trying—is based on the assumption that he must ultimately fail. He believes that Snowden's gory death revealed a secret: that man is, ultimately, garbage. The

specter of death haunts Yossarian constantly, in forms ranging from the dead man in his tent to his memories of Snowden. Furthermore, Yossarian is always visualizing his own death and is absolutely flabbergasted by the total number of ways in which it is possible for a human being to die. But Yossarian's awareness of the inevitability of death is not entirely negative: it gives him a sense of how precious life is, after all, and he vows to live for as long as possible. He also lives more fully than he would without his constant consciousness of life's frailty. He falls in love constantly and passionately, and he laments every second that he cannot spend enjoying the good things in the world.

MOTIFS

Motifs are recurring structures, contrasts, or literary devices that can help to develop and inform the text's major themes.

CATCH-22
One version of Catch-22 keeps Yossarian flying combat mission after combat mission: Doc Daneeka cannot ground him for insanity unless he asks, but if he asks to be grounded, then he must be sane. In this sense, Catch-22 is a piece of circular reasoning that keeps Yossarian trapped in a paradox that determines whether he lives or dies, even though it is made only of words. But Catch-22 has many other permutations, most notably in the final, general principle stated by the old Italian woman in the ruined brothel: "they have a right to do anything we can't stop them from doing." This description of Catch-22 proves what Yossarian has known all along: Catch-22 does not really exist. It is just a name made up for an illogical argument that justifies what is really going on. Behind Catch-22 stands an unswerving principle: might makes right.

Catch-22 also manifests itself even when it is not explicitly named. Both the doctor and the chaplain have been caught up in their own versions of Catch-22, since war drastically undermines the premises of their professions and yet calls upon them to practice those professions in the name of war. Even Heller's style is in a way a Catch-22; the dialogue leaps haphazardly from one comment to another, often arriving at a point exactly opposite of that which the person speaking is trying to express.

NUMBER OF MISSIONS
Colonel Cathcart wants to be promoted to general; to gain promotion, he constantly raises the number of missions that the men are

required to fly before they can be discharged. The number of missions increases as time goes on, providing us with one of the few ways we have of keeping track of the chronology of *Catch*-22. The number of missions is also the primary trap from which the men in the squadron are unable to escape: each time Hungry Joe completes his missions or Yossarian comes near completing them, the number is raised yet again. The utter futility of trying to get out of the system the honest way, by flying the required number of missions, is what prompts Orr and Yossarian to seek alternative methods of escape.

WASHINGTON IRVING

First signed as a forgery by Yossarian in the hospital, the name Washington Irving (or Irving Washington) is soon adopted by Major Major, who signs the name because the paperwork with Irving's name on it never comes back to him. Washington Irving is a figment of the imagination who is, in a sense, the perfect person to deal with bureaucracy: because he does not exist, he is ideally suited to the meaningless shuffle of paperwork.

SYMBOLS

Symbols are objects, characters, figures, or colors used to represent abstract ideas or concepts.

CHOCOLATE-COVERED COTTON

Aided by Yossarian, Milo comes up with the idea of selling chocolate-covered cotton to the government after he discovers that there is a glut of cotton in the market and that he cannot sell his own cotton. Milo's product hides the lack of substance beneath an enticing exterior, showing the way in which bureaucracy can be fooled by appearances and is unable to measure actual substance or real merit.

THE SOLDIER IN WHITE

The soldier in white, a bandage-wrapped, faceless, nameless body that lies in the hospital in the first chapter of the novel, represents the way the army treats men as interchangeable objects. When, months after his death, he is replaced by another, identical soldier in white, everyone assumes it is the same person.

AERIAL PHOTOGRAPHS

When the men go on bombing missions, they often later learn that the real purpose of the mission was either to make an explosion that would be beautiful when it showed up on aerial photographs or to clear out foliage so that better aerial photography will be possible. The photographs themselves, then, stand for the way in which the dehumanization of war—in this case, the detachment of the upper levels of military bureaucracy from the tragedy of war—allows for its horrors to be seen merely for their aesthetic effects.

SYMBOLS

Summary & Analysis

Chapters 1–5

Summary — Chapter 1: The Texan

Not wanting to face the violence of World War II, Yossarian, an American soldier, has gone to an Italian military hospital claiming to have a pain in his liver. The doctors seem unable to prove that he is well, so they let him stay, though they are perplexed that his condition is neither improving nor worsening. The hospital patients are required to censor letters traveling between the soldiers and their loved ones at home. Yossarian plays games with the letters, deleting words according to his own arbitrary rules and affixing his signature as "Washington Irving." He shares the hospital ward with his friend Dunbar, a bandaged, immobile man called "the soldier in white," and a pair of nurses who appear to hate Yossarian.

An affable Texan is admitted to the ward one day, and the Texan tries to convince the patients that "decent folk" deserve extra votes. The Texan's patriotism deeply annoys the other patients. Meanwhile, a chaplain comes to see Yossarian, who enjoys the chaplain's company. But within ten days of the Texan's arrival at the hospital, almost everyone, including Yossarian, flees the ward out of annoyance with the Texan, recovering from his or her ailments and returning to active duty.

Summary — Chapter 2: Clevinger

When he leaves the hospital, Yossarian feels that he is the only one concerned about the senseless war in which millions of young men are bombing each other. He remembers arguing about the nature of the war with an officer in his group named Clevinger. Yossarian had claimed that everyone was trying to kill him, while Clevinger argued that no one was trying to kill Yossarian personally. Yossarian had rejected Clevinger's arguments about countries and honor; for Yossarian, the salient fact was that people kept shooting at him.

Yossarian sees his roommate, Orr, and finds out that Clevinger is still missing. He remembers the last time he and Clevinger called each other crazy, during a night at the officers' club when Yossarian announced to everyone present that he was superhuman because no one had managed to kill him yet. Yossarian is suspicious of everyone when he gets out of the hospital. He has a delicious meal in Milo's gourmet mess hall, then talks to Doc Daneeka, who enrages Yossarian by telling him that Colonel Cathcart has raised the number of missions required before a soldier can be discharged from forty-five to fifty. At the time of this change, Yossarian had flown forty-four missions.

SUMMARY — CHAPTER 3: HAVERMEYER

Orr tells Yossarian a nonsensical story about how he liked to stuff crab apples in his cheeks when he was younger. Yossarian briefly remembers an episode in Rome during which a whore beat Orr over the head with her shoe. Yossarian reflects on Orr's size; he is even smaller than Huple, a young boy who lives near Hungry Joe's tent. Hungry Joe has nightmares whenever he is not scheduled to fly a mission the next day, and his screaming keeps the whole camp awake. Hungry Joe's tent is near a road where the men sometimes pick up girls and take them out to the tall grass across the road from an open-air movie theater.

A U.S.O. (United Service Organizations) troupe that visited the theater that afternoon has been sent by an ambitious general named P. P. Peckem, who hopes to take over the command of Yossarian's unit from General Dreedle. General Peckem's troubleshooter, Colonel Cargill, used to be a marketing executive paid by Wall Street firms to fail at marketing so that they could establish tax losses. Cargill does much the same thing now as a colonel: he fails most notably at bringing enthusiasm to the men, some of whom have finished their fifty missions and anxiously hope their orders to return home arrive before Colonel Cathcart raises the number of missions again.

Yossarian feels sick, but Doc Daneeka refuses to ground him. Doc Daneeka advises Yossarian to emulate Havermeyer, a fearless bombardier, and make the best of his situation. But Yossarian thinks that his fear is healthy. The narrator notes that Havermeyer likes to shoot mice in the middle of the night and that he once woke Hungry Joe with a shot that compelled him to dive into a slit trench. These slit trenches had mysteriously appeared beside every tent the morning following the mess officer Milo Minderbinder's bombing of the squadron.

SUMMARY — CHAPTER 4: DOC DANEEKA

The narrator explains that Hungry Joe is crazy and thus Yossarian is trying to give him advice. Hungry Joe won't listen, however, because he thinks Yossarian is crazy. Doc Daneeka, in turn, tells Yossarian that his own problems are worse than Hungry Joe's because the war has interrupted his lucrative medical practice.

Yossarian remembers trying to disrupt the educational meeting in Captain Black's intelligence tent by asking unanswerable questions, which caused Group Headquarters to make a rule that the only people who could ask questions were the ones who never did. This rule comes from Colonel Cathcart and Lieutenant Colonel Korn. These two colonels also approved the construction of a skeet-shooting range at which Yossarian never hits anything. Dunbar, though, shoots skeet frequently because he hates it. Dunbar believes that when he engages in activities that are boring or uncomfortable, time passes more slowly and he thereby lengthens his life. He argues with Clevinger about this theory. Meanwhile, ex-P.F.C. Wintergreen has started a panic among the officers in Rome by telephoning them and saying only, "T. S. Eliot." Although he intends these words as a response to a general memo from a colonel saying that it would be hard to name a poet who makes any money, General Peckem assumes that the words constitute a coded message and suffers great anxiety as a result.

SUMMARY — CHAPTER 5: CHIEF WHITE HALFOAT

> *There was only one catch and that was Catch-22, which*
> *specified that a concern for one's own safety . . . was the*
> *process of a rational mind.*
> *(See* QUOTATIONS, *p. 53)*

In the tent that Doc Daneeka and an alcoholic Native American named Chief White Halfoat share, Doc Daneeka describes his corrupt Staten Island medical practice to Yossarian. He tells him about some sexually inept newlyweds who once visited his office. Chief White Halfoat enters, telling Yossarian that Doc Daneeka is crazy. Halfoat then relates the story of his own family: because every place that he and his family settled turned out to be on top of a significant oil supply, major oil companies began following them, using them as "human divining rods." The oil companies then kicked them off the land, forcing the family to live a nomadic life.

Yossarian again pleads with Doc Daneeka to be grounded, asking if he would be grounded if he were crazy. Doc Daneeka replies that he would, and Yossarian argues that he is indeed crazy. Doc Daneeka then describes Catch-22, a regulation holding that, in order to be grounded for insanity, a pilot must ask to be grounded;

but any pilot who asks to be grounded must be sane, since sane people would never want to fly bombing missions. Impressed, Yossarian takes Doc Daneeka's word for it, just as he had taken Orr's word about the flies in Appleby's eyes: Orr had insisted that there are flies in Appleby's eyes, and though Yossarian had no idea what Orr meant, he believed him because Orr had never lied to him before.

Yossarian begins thinking about bombing missions and how much he hates his position in the nose of the plane, where he is separated from the escape hatch by a passage just wide enough to fit through. On these bombing missions, Yossarian is always terrified for his life, and he pleads with the pilot, McWatt, to avoid antiaircraft fire. He remembers one mission when, while the squadron was taking evasive action, Dobbs, the co-pilot, went crazy and started screaming, "Help him." The plane spun out of control and Yossarian believed he was going to die. Enigmatically, the narrator states that someone named Snowden lay dying in the back of the plane.

ANALYSIS — CHAPTERS 1–5

One of the main goals of *Catch-22* is to satirize the dehumanizing machinery of war by showing the irremovable survival impulse at the heart of every individual. By constantly making fun of wartime situations and by carrying arguments to their extreme, absurd conclusions, the novel shows the conflict that arises when a war's course is determined by factors alien to the people who are fighting the war. Through a maze of characters and events, *Catch-22* explores war and bureaucracy and their effects on ordinary people.

In these early chapters, these effects take the form of an absurd irony that penetrates virtually every facet of the characters' lives. The greatest irony is, of course, the perceived uselessness of the war—at least as it is carried out by the characters who surround Yossarian. All that matters to the generals controlling the troops is getting a promotion; all that matters to the troops is staying alive long enough to go home. No one is concerned with the larger political or ethical implications of the war. This grand irony is played out in hundreds of small ways, with Yossarian and his companions acting in self-defeating, paradoxical ways simply because their actions have so little meaning. In the hospital, for example, Yossarian and his companions hate the Texan because he is so likable, and Yossarian makes a fool of the chaplain even though he senselessly loves him. Furthermore, wielded with wickedly satirical intent, the banter between characters is full of paradoxes as impossible as Catch-22 itself.

One of the statements that the novel makes is that the rules that govern individuals also tend to shape their thoughts. The early chapters show us how the soldiers, imprisoned by the paradox of Catch-22, take this type of paradox to heart, pursuing irrelevancy, meaninglessness, and nonsense as though they are real values in a world where relevancy, meaning, and sense are impossible. The power of bureaucracy further manifests itself in the first few chapters through Colonel Cathcart's impersonal raising of the number of required missions and even more through Doc Daneeka's explanation of Catch-22—Yossarian is forced to confront the revelation that the law governing his life is an irresolvable paradox.

The failure of communication plays an important role in the development of Heller's paradoxes. Words have little meaning, a truth that becomes clear in the very first chapter as Yossarian capriciously deletes random words from letters simply because he finds the letters boring. Heller often uses miscommunication to create comedy, as when ex-P.F.C. Wintergreen causes General Peckem a great deal of worry by calling him and saying, "T. S. Eliot"—a simple, harmless phrase that Peckem interprets as something complicated and sinister. Part of the irony here is that insubstantial, easily misinterpreted words are what determine the very real, substantial aspects of the soldiers' lives. The contrast between the actual fighting and the ridiculous bureaucracy that controls it is one of the most horrifying aspects of *Catch-22*.

Finally, even the notion of time itself is affected by the absurdity governing characters' lives. The story is told with a jumbled chronology involving recollections, allusions to future events, and statements whose meanings become clear only as the novel progresses. The narrative skips from scene to scene with occasional (but still confusing) mentions of *before* and *after* but with no central *now* to give these terms meaning. However, a number of handholds are offered to enable us to put the events in some kind of order: the growth of Milo's syndicate, the ranks of certain officers, and, most important, the number of missions the men are expected to fly.

CHAPTERS 6–10

SUMMARY — CHAPTER 6: HUNGRY JOE
Although Hungry Joe has already flown his fifty missions, the orders to send him home never come, and he continues to scream at

night. Doc Daneeka ignores Hungry Joe's problems and instead complains about having been forced to leave his clinic. Hungry Joe is mad with lust; his desperate attempts to take pictures of naked women always end in failure, as the pictures do not come out. In order to get women to pose for him, Hungry Joe pretends to be an important *Life* magazine photographer—ironically, he really was a photographer for *Life* before the war. Hungry Joe has flown six tours of duty, but every time he finishes one, Colonel Cathcart raises the number of missions required before Hungry Joe can be sent home. With each increase in the minimum number of missions, Hungry Joe's nightmares stop until he finishes another tour. The narrator tells us that Colonel Cathcart is very brave about volunteering his men for the most dangerous missions.

Appleby, another member of the squadron, is equally brave in his Ping-Pong games. One night, Orr, Yossarian's roommate, attacks Appleby in the middle of a game. A fight breaks out, and Chief White Halfoat breaks the nose of Colonel Moodus, General Dreedle's son-in-law. General Dreedle so enjoys witnessing this abuse of his son-in-law that he keeps calling Chief White Halfoat in to repeat the performance and moves him into Doc Daneeka's tent to make sure that Halfoat remains in top physical condition.

Ex-P.F.C. Wintergreen gives Yossarian another definition of Catch-22, one that requires him to fly the extra missions that Colonel Cathcart orders, even though Twenty-seventh Air Force regulations demand only forty missions. The reasoning is that the regulations state also that Yossarian must obey all of Cathcart's orders, and Cathcart has raised the number of missions again, this time to fifty-five.

SUMMARY — CHAPTER 7: McWATT

McWatt, Yossarian's pilot, manages to display a cheeriness in the face of war, even though he is perfectly sane. This contradiction leads Yossarian to believe that McWatt, who is smiling and polite and who loves to whistle show tunes, is the "craziest combat man" in the unit.

Yossarian gets a letter from Doc Daneeka about his liver that orders the mess hall to give Yossarian all the fresh fruit he wants. Nervous that his liver will improve—which would mean having to leave the hospital—Yossarian refuses to eat the fruit. Milo, however, tries to persuade Yossarian to sell the fruit on the black market, but Yossarian refuses. Milo explains to Yossarian his desire to serve the best meals in the entire world in his mess hall and his nervousness about his chef, Corporal Snark, who poisoned his entire previous squadron by putting GI soap in the sweet potatoes.

Milo becomes indignant when he learns that a C.I.D. (Criminal Investigation Division) man is searching for a criminal who has been forging Washington Irving's name in censored letters. He thinks the investigation is a ploy to expose him for selling items on the black market. Milo wants to organize the men into a syndicate, a concept that he tries to explain to Yossarian by stealing McWatt's bedsheet, ripping it into pieces, and redistributing it. Yossarian does not understand Milo's version of economics, which largely involves cheating whomever he is trading with and then claiming moral superiority.

Summary — Chapter 8: Lieutenant Scheisskopf

[N]owhere in the world, not in all the fascist tanks or planes or submarines ... were there men who hated him more.

(See QUOTATIONS, p. 53)

Clevinger does not understand Milo's plan either, even though he usually understands everything about the war except for the arbitrary way in which things happen. Yossarian remembers training in America with Clevinger under Lieutenant Scheisskopf, who had been obsessed with parades, and whose wife, along with her friend Dori Duz, had slept with all the men under her husband's command. Lieutenant Scheisskopf hates Clevinger and finally gets him sent to trial under a belligerent colonel. At the trial, Clevinger is unable to communicate his innocence because he is harangued about using improper modes of address. Clevinger is extremely confused by his superiors' hatred of him; he realizes that Lieutenant Scheisskopf and the colonel harbor an animosity toward him that no enemy soldier ever could.

Summary — Chapter 9: Major Major Major Major

The narrator explains the details of Major Major Major's troubled childhood. His unfortunate name is a result of his father's twisted sense of humor and causes Major much distress throughout his youth. Major also bears a strong resemblance to Henry Fonda, upon which people constantly comment, and he does so well in school as a child that the FBI monitors him on suspicion that he is a communist. His troubles continue when an IBM computer error makes him a major the day he joins the army, resulting in his new name, Major Major Major Major. His sudden promotion stuns his drill sergeant, who then has to train a man who is suddenly his superior officer. Luckily, Major Major applies for aviation cadet training and is sent away to Lieutenant Scheisskopf, who is himself confused about how to interact with an officer who outranks him but to whom he is a commanding officer. Scheisskopf trains Major quickly in order to get rid of him, and sends him to Pianosa, where Yossarian's squadron is stationed. Not long after arriving in Pianosa, where Major is happy for the first time in his life, he is made squadron commander by a vengeful Colonel Cathcart. As a result, Major loses all his friends, who become servile in his presence.

Major Major has always been a drab, mediocre sort of person and has never had friends before; he lapses into an awkward depression and refuses to be seen in his office. To make himself feel better, Major Major forges Washington Irving's name on official documents. He is confused about everything, including his official relationship to Major —— de Coverley, his executive officer: he does not know whether he is Major —— de Coverley's subordinate or vice versa. A C.I.D. man comes to investigate the Washington Irving scandal, but Major Major denies knowledge of it. The incompetent C.I.D. man believes him—as does another C.I.D. man who arrives shortly thereafter, then leaves to investigate the first C.I.D. man. Major Major starts wearing dark glasses and a false mustache when forging Washington Irving's name; he even forges a few "John Milton" signatures, just for variety. One day, Yossarian tackles Major Major and demands to be grounded. Major Major sadly tells Yossarian that there is nothing he can do.

SUMMARY — CHAPTER 10: WINTERGREEN

Clevinger's plane disappears in a cloud off the coast of Elba, and he is presumed dead. Yossarian, however, is unable to conceive of Clevinger's death, and instead assumes that he is simply, and inexplicably, missing. The narrator then describes ex-P.F.C. Wintergreen's past: back in the U.S., ex-P.F.C. Wintergreen continually goes AWOL. He is required to dig holes and fill them up again as punishment—work he approaches as a duty to his country. One day, ex-P.F.C. Wintergreen nicks a water pipe, and water sprays everywhere. Since Chief White Halfoat is with Wintergreen, everyone assumes that it is oil, and Halfoat and Wintergreen are both sent away to Pianosa.

Yossarian recalls Mudd, a soldier who had arrived at the camp and died in combat before even reporting for duty. Nobody can actually remember Mudd, but his belongings remain in Yossarian's tent and seem to be "contaminated with death." This reminder of death causes Yossarian to think about the deadly mission of the Great Big Siege of Bologna, for which Colonel Cathcart had bravely volunteered his men. At the time, not even sick men could be grounded by doctors. One of the doctors, Dr. Stubbs, asked cynically what point there was to saving lives when everyone was going to die anyway. Dunbar replied that the point was to live as long as possible and forget about the fact that death was inevitable.

ANALYSIS — CHAPTERS 6–10

In these chapters, many of the novel's characters begin to accept the futility and illogic of the actions that the army and higher levels of bureaucracy demand of those involved in the war effort. First among those who resign themselves to the absurdity is Major Major Major Major, one of the most comical and improbable characters in the novel: all his life, Major Major has been the victim of bureaucratic forces beyond his control—his birth certificate, the IBM machine—and he eventually turns on these forces by forging false names on official documents. The way in which he rebels against the system reflects both his own dissatisfaction with his ludicrous name, which bureaucracy has generated, and the reliance upon names, cataloging, and indexing perpetuated by the bureaucracy. Major —— de Coverley is another ridiculous and paradoxical figure, a revered old man with no important duties who plays horseshoes all day and is utterly irrelevant to the war. Actions, too, can be irrelevant and nonsensical: ex-P.F.C. Wintergreen's punishment for going AWOL is to dig holes and then fill them back up again. Wintergreen says that he doesn't mind doing it, so long as it is "part of the war effort." Obviously, his task is not helping the Allies win the war; its uselessness suggests that so many other actions that the army seems to believe are necessary are actually a waste of time. A similar sense of futility occurs with Major Major's realization that the documents he signs keep coming back to him for more signatures. His life is consumed with paperwork that repeats itself in an endless cycle in which nothing gets accomplished.

Catch-22's mosaic of anecdotes, whose chronological placement remains largely beyond the reader's grasp, undermines the conventional model of various events building tension toward a climax. It also conveys the impression that, just as Yossarian is afraid to confront a life that ends in death, the novel itself is nervous about the passing of time, which leads inevitably toward death. Breaking up the flow of time is, in a sense, a narrative attempt to defy mortality. In these early chapters, Dunbar presents an important alternative to this approach: he knows he is trapped in linear time, but he hopes to live in it as long as possible by making time move more slowly in his perception. He thus seeks boredom and discomfort because time seems to pass more slowly when he is bored or uncomfortable. This separation of the actual passage of time from the experience of time is an attempt to regain control of a life constantly threatened by the violence of war.

The novel's exploration of this quirky passing of time demonstrates how the novel's satirical and serious tones complement each other. Dunbar's argument about doing unpleasant things because they make time pass more slowly, a statement that seems entirely illogical and even comical the first time we read it, begins to make sense as the novel progresses. The only way in which these soldiers are able to approach the ludicrous situation in which they have been placed is to indulge their own ludicrous logic. Dr. Stubbs's frustrated reflection in Chapter 10 that the arbitrary nature of death makes it absurd to try to live makes Dunbar's ideas about making time last longer seem somewhat logical: a response to the possibility of imminent death that espouses self-preservation is no longer comical but rather completely rational.

Part of the reason for Yossarian's terror of death is that he has no control over his own fate. Again and again, the impersonal machine that seems to be running the war in *Catch*-22 denies characters the ability to shape their own destinies. The law of Catch-22 seems to be the embodiment of this trap: even when soldiers can think of rational reasons to go home from the war, Catch-22 always stops them. A large part of the powerlessness the men feel comes from the bureaucratic regulations that prevent rational action; the men's actions are guided by rules that have little to do with reality. The hilarious conversations that result from attempting to stick to the rules are often pitiful because they highlight how inhuman the bureaucracy is. In Chapter 8, for example, Scheisskopf's haranguing of Clevinger about the mode of his address when Clevinger attempts to communicate his innocence demonstrates how Scheisskopf focuses only on superficial things, such as matters of propriety, and completely ignores substantial things, such as his men's individual needs and feelings.

CHAPTERS 11–16

SUMMARY — CHAPTER 11: CAPTAIN BLACK

Captain Black is pleased to hear that Colonel Cathcart has volunteered the men for the lethal mission of bombing Bologna. Captain Black hates the men and gloats about their terrifying, violent task. He is extremely ambitious and had hoped to be promoted to squadron commander, but when Major Major is picked over him, he lapses into a deep depression, out of which the Bologna mission lifts him. Captain Black tries to get revenge on Major Major by initiating the Glorious Loyalty Oath Crusade, during which he forces all the men to swear elaborate oaths of loyalty before doing basic things like eating meals. He then refuses to let Major Major sign a loyalty oath and hopes, thereby, to make him appear disloyal. The Glorious Loyalty Oath Crusade is a major event in the camp until the fearsome Major —— de Coverley puts an end to it by hollering "Gimme eat!" in the mess hall without signing an oath.

SUMMARY — CHAPTER 12: BOLOGNA

It rains interminably before the Bologna mission, and the bombing run is delayed. The men all hope it will never stop raining. When it does, Yossarian moves the bomb line on the map so that the commanding officers will think that Bologna has already been captured. Yossarian also gives the entire squadron diarrhea by poisoning the food so that they won't have to fly. The rain then starts again.

In the meantime, ex-P.F.C. Wintergreen tries to sell Yossarian a cigarette lighter, going into competition with Milo as a black-market trader. He is aghast that Milo has cornered the entire world market for Egyptian cotton but is unable to sell any of it. The men are terrified and miserable about having to bomb Bologna. Clevinger and Yossarian argue about whether it is Yossarian's duty to bomb Bologna, and, by the middle of the second week of waiting, everyone in the squadron is as emaciated as Hungry Joe.

One night, Yossarian, Nately, and Dunbar go for a drunken drive with Chief White Halfoat; they crash a jeep and realize that it has stopped raining. Back in the tents, Hungry Joe is trying to shoot Huple's cat, which has been giving him nightmares, and the men force Hungry Joe to fight the cat fairly. The cat runs away, and Hungry Joe is satisfied. When he goes back to sleep, however, he has another nightmare about the cat.

SUMMARY — CHAPTER 13: MAJOR — — DE COVERLEY

Major —— de Coverley is a daunting, majestic man with a lion's mane of white hair, an eagle's gaze, and a transparent eye patch. Everyone is afraid of him, and no one will talk to him. His sole duty is traveling to major cities captured by the Americans to rent rooms in which his men can take leave; he spends the rest of his time playing horseshoes. Major —— de Coverley always manages to be photographed with the first wave of American troops moving into a city, a fact that perplexes both the enemy and the American commanders. He seems to be a force of nature, and yet Yossarian is able to fool him by moving the bomb line: Major —— de Coverley has traveled to enemy-controlled Bologna and has not yet returned. The narrator relates that Milo once approached —— de Coverley on the horseshoe range, successfully requesting authorization to import eggs on Air Force planes.

We also learn that Colonel Cathcart had attempted to give Yossarian a medal some time earlier. When Yossarian was brave, he had circled over a target twice in order to hit it, and, on the second pass, Kraft, a younger pilot from the division, had been killed by shrapnel. Not knowing how to rebuke Yossarian for his foolhardiness, the authorities decided to stave off criticism by giving him a medal.

SUMMARY — CHAPTER 14: KID SAMPSON

The squadron finally receives the go-ahead to bomb Bologna, but by this time Yossarian does not feel like going over the target even once. He pretends that his plane's intercom system is broken and orders his pilot, Kid Sampson, to turn back. They land at the deserted airfield just before dawn, feeling strangely morose. Yossarian takes a nap on the beach and wakes up when the planes fly back. Not a single plane has been hit. Yossarian thinks that cloud cover must have prevented them from bombing the city and that they will have to make another attempt, but he is wrong: facing no antiaircraft fire, the Americans bombed the city without incurring any losses.

SUMMARY — CHAPTER 15: PILTCHARD & WREN

Captain Piltchard and Captain Wren ineffectually reprimand Yossarian and his crew for turning back and inform the men that since they missed the ammunition dumps the first time, they will have to bomb Bologna again. Yossarian confidently flies in, assuming there will be no antiaircraft fire, and he is stunned when shrapnel begins firing up toward him through the skies. He furiously directs McWatt into evasive maneuvers and fights with the strangely cheerful Aarfy until the bombs are dropped. Yossarian does not die—though many other men in the squadron do—and the plane lands safely. Yossarian heads immediately for emergency rest leave in Rome.

SUMMARY — CHAPTER 16: LUCIANA

Luciana is a beautiful Italian woman whom Yossarian meets at a bar in Rome. After he buys her dinner and dances with her, she agrees to sleep with him, but not right then—she will come to his room the next morning. She does, but then angrily refuses to sleep with Yossarian until she cleans his room, disgustedly calling him a pig. Finally, she lets him sleep with her. Afterward, Yossarian falls in love with her and asks her to marry him. She says she won't marry him because he is crazy; she knows he is crazy because no one in his right mind would marry a girl who was not a virgin. She tells him about a scar she got when the Americans bombed her town.

Suddenly, Hungry Joe rushes in with his camera, and Yossarian and Luciana have to get dressed. Laughing, they go outside, where they part ways. Luciana gives Yossarian her number, telling him that she expects him to tear it up as soon as she leaves because she thinks that he is impressed with himself that such a pretty girl would sleep with him for free. He asks her why on earth he would do such a thing. As soon as she leaves, though, Yossarian, impressed with himself that such a pretty girl would sleep with him for free, tears up her number. Almost immediately he regrets doing so, and, after learning that Colonel Cathcart has raised the number of missions to forty, he makes the anguished decision to go straight to the hospital.

ANALYSIS — CHAPTERS 11–16

In this section, the disordered chronology functions as an instrument for building suspense. The lengthy digression about the Great Loyalty Oath Crusade interrupts the tense build-up to the Bologna mission, which occurs shortly before the scene at the beginning of the novel, when the number of required missions is still thirty-five. The Great Loyalty Oath Crusade story is ironic and funny; the Bologna mission is a dismal story told in terms of endless rain and growing worry. By breaking off the Bologna story in the middle to tell the exaggerated parable of the Loyalty Oath Crusade, Heller heightens the sense of uncertainty and anticipation surrounding the outcome of the Bologna mission. During the description of the actual bombing run to Bologna, however, Heller devotes a chapter almost entirely to a single event, without his usual digressions. This very detailed, vivid account of the attack makes time appear to move more slowly, trapping the reader in the same drawn-out terror as the characters. The earnest, straightforward manner in which the Bologna story is told is a signal that we are meant to take this episode seriously—that there is nothing funny about this aspect of war.

Although *Catch-22* is written mostly from the perspective of a third-person narrator who describes what each of the characters is thinking, we hear mostly what is happening in Yossarian's mind, and many of the observations about the absurdity of the war seem to be his own. So, despite the fact that each chapter of *Catch-22* bears the name of a character described in that chapter, the narrative generally returns to Yossarian. A significant departure from this organizational method occurs in the chapter entitled "Bologna," however: instead of operating as a largely humorous description of the nature and history of one of the novel's characters, this chapter remains almost entirely in the present of the story, and Yossarian is forced to confront his desire to live at the expense of everything else. The chapter title itself—a place name rather than a person's name—marks a shift from a satirical and humorous focus on the unwitting characters engaged in the war to a serious focus on the present realities of the war.

Yossarian's vague guilt about abandoning his friends reveals a weakness in his philosophy of self-preservation: he seems to have no qualms about abandoning the mission and thereby keeping himself alive, but he does care about his friends and feels a mild trepidation while he awaits their return. Up to this point, Yossarian's sole goal in life has been survival at the expense of everything else: he has subjected himself and his squadron to various illnesses, refused to enjoy fruit because it might make him healthy, and endured rather unpleasant hospital stays—all for the sake of not having to fly missions. Yossarian faces a difficult dilemma: on one hand, caring for others is destructive in that it undermines his ability to try to save his own life; on the other hand, caring for others is the only thing that mitigates the impersonal hatred that Yossarian perceives directed toward him.

The interlude with Luciana provides a welcome respite from life in the camp on Pianosa, but it also illustrates the strain placed on male-female relationships by the war. Luciana and Yossarian seem legitimately drawn to one another, but their relationship is brief and almost wholly sexual. Hungry Joe's interruption of their time together demonstrates the glaring lack of privacy in Yossarian's life and highlights the difficulty of having meaningful relationships in wartime. Similarly, Yossarian's tearing up of Luciana's number constitutes an act of irrational, self-satisfied exuberance that seems part and parcel of the absurd ironies forced on him by the Catch-22 mentality of the war. He is so overwhelmed at the end of this section—after Bologna, after Luciana, and after he learns that the number of missions has been raised yet again—that he decides to check into the hospital, a place of relative sanity and safety.

CHAPTERS 17–21

SUMMARY — CHAPTER 17: THE SOLDIER IN WHITE

He wondered often how he would ever recognize ... the
vocal slip, loss of balance or lapse of memory
that would signal the inevitable beginning of the
inevitable end.

(See QUOTATIONS, p. 54)

Yossarian has returned to the hospital, where he finds life (and death) more palatable than in his recurring memories of being on a bomb run with Snowden dying in the back, whispering, "I'm cold." At the hospital, death is orderly and polite, and there is no inexplicable violence. Dunbar is in the hospital with Yossarian, and they are both perplexed by the soldier in white, a man completely covered in plaster bandages. The men in the hospital discuss the injustice of mortality—some men are killed and some are not, and some men get sick and some do not, without any pattern or logic. Some time earlier, Clevinger had tried to explain why there might be some justice in such illogical deaths, but Yossarian was too busy keeping track of all the forces trying to kill him to listen. Later, Yossarian and Hungry Joe collect lists of fatal diseases that they can claim to have. Doc Daneeka, however, frequently refuses to ground them even when they claim to have these diseases. The doctor tells Yossarian that after Yossarian flies his fifty-five missions he will think about helping Yossarian.

SUMMARY — CHAPTER 18: THE SOLDIER WHO SAW EVERYTHING TWICE

The first time Yossarian ever goes to the hospital, he is still a private. He feigns an abdominal pain, but when the doctors decide he has been cured, he pretends to have the mysterious ailment of another soldier in the ward who says he "sees everything twice." He spends Thanksgiving in the hospital and vows to spend all future Thanksgivings there, but he breaks that oath when he spends the next Thanksgiving in bed with Lieutenant Scheisskopf's wife, arguing about God. After Yossarian claims he is cured of seeing everything twice, he is asked to pretend to be a dying soldier whose mother, father, and brother have come to visit him. The family, which has traveled to visit their family member, does not know that he died that morning. The doctors bandage Yossarian, who pretends to be the dying soldier. The soldier's father asks Yossarian to tell God that it is not right for men to die so young.

SUMMARY — CHAPTER 19: COLONEL CATHCART

> *Haven't you got anything humorous that stays away*
> *from . . . God? I'd like to keep away from the subject of*
> *religion altogether if we can.*
>
> *(See* QUOTATIONS, *p. 55)*

The ambitious Colonel Cathcart browbeats the chaplain, demanding a prayer before each bombing run, an idea he takes from the *Saturday Evening Post*. He then abandons the idea after the chaplain suggests that God might punish them for not including the enlisted men. The chaplain timidly mentions that some of the men have complained about Colonel Cathcart's habit of raising the number of missions required every few weeks, but Colonel Cathcart ignores him.

SUMMARY — CHAPTER 20: CORPORAL WHITCOMB

On his way home, the chaplain meets Colonel Korn, Colonel Cathcart's wily, cynical sidekick. Colonel Korn mocks Colonel Cathcart in front of the chaplain and is highly suspicious of a plum tomato that Colonel Cathcart offered the chaplain. At his tent in the woods, the chaplain encounters the hostile Corporal Whitcomb, his atheistic assistant, who resents him deeply for holding back his career. Corporal Whitcomb tells the chaplain that a C.I.D. man suspects the chaplain of signing Washington Irving's name to official papers and of stealing plum tomatoes. The poor chaplain is very unhappy, because he feels helpless to improve anyone's life.

SUMMARY — CHAPTER 21: GENERAL DREEDLE

Colonel Cathcart has become preoccupied with Yossarian's behavior—particularly his complaints about the number of required missions and the fact that he appeared naked at his medal ceremony shortly after Snowden's death. Yossarian had refused to wear clothes to the ceremony because Snowden, dying in the back of the plane, had bled all over him, and Yossarian never wanted to wear a uniform again. Yossarian is also responsible for a moaning epidemic at the briefing before the Avignon mission during which Snowden was killed; he started moaning because the mission's dangers meant that he might never again sleep with a beautiful woman.

Colonel Cathcart wishes he knew how to solve the problem posed by Yossarian's mischief, for this would impress General Dreedle, Cathcart's commanding officer. General Dreedle, however, does not care what his men do, as long as they remain alive in reliable military quantities. He travels everywhere with a buxom nurse and worries mostly about Colonel Moodus, his son-in-law, whom he despises and thus occasionally asks Chief White Halfoat to punch in the nose. The narrator relates that Colonel Korn once tried to undercut Colonel Cathcart by giving a flamboyant briefing to impress General Dreedle; General Dreedle, unimpressed, told Colonel Cathcart that Colonel Korn made him sick.

ANALYSIS — CHAPTERS 17–21

In *Catch-22,* the hospital is certainly not a place where heroic doctors heal grateful patients, but Yossarian's ridiculous experience in this chapter goes so far as to parody the idea of a hospital as a place where death can be confronted and properly mourned. For Yossarian, the hospital is nothing more than a refuge from the atrocities that occur outside its walls, and he is unable to understand why a family would want to arrive at a hospital to watch their son die. The hospital staff further parodies the hospital as a site of grief by requesting that Yossarian pretend to be a dying soldier for the sake of a family whose real son has already passed away. Adding somber draperies and stinking flowers to the room, the hospital is as unable as the rest of the bureaucracy to take death seriously, and the family members who do mourn their son or brother's passing are comically portrayed as overly sentimental. While one might expect that a war would underline the fragility of life and make those involved appreciate ritual celebrations of life and mourning of death all the more, in *Catch-22* the war numbs these characters to the effects of death, which has become a mundane, daily occurrence. As a result, the actions of those who still take death seriously are incomprehensible or meaningless to those involved in the war. Heller's statement, however, is *not* that life is meaningless; it would be a mistake to assume that Yossarian's attitude or the doctors' attitudes toward death are Heller's own. Rather, it seems that the novel's purpose in displaying such an unconventional portrait of mourning is to show the absurd behavior that war forces humans to adopt—reaching a point where not even the loss of life is impressive.

In one of the novel's manifold contradictions, two atheists, Yossarian and Mrs. Scheisskopf, argue over what kind of God they do not believe in and address the nature of God in a debate. The God in whom Mrs. Scheisskopf does not believe is good and all-knowing, whereas Yossarian's deity is bumbling and confused. Yossarian's argument is typical: that a truly compassionate God would not have allowed all the unpleasantness and pain in the world. But the details that Yossarian uses to argue his point are unusual: he asks why God would create phlegm, tooth decay, or incontinence. Yossarian is not just angry with the God that he does not believe in, but he also ridicules him. Mrs. Scheisskopf, on the other hand, prefers not to believe in a good and righteous God, arguing that if one is not going to believe in God, one might as well not believe in a good God. In this way, the idea of God can be useful, even if it is not accurate. The contrast between the chaplain and his assistant, the atheist Corporal Whitcomb, further develops this paradox. The chaplain, who does believe in God, has a very quiet, nonintrusive manner as he ministers to the men in the squadron, which does not turn many men toward religion. Corporal Whitcomb, on the other hand, wants to enter into a full-scale religious campaign, which would include revivals and form letters sent from the chaplain to the families of men killed in combat. Like Mrs. Scheisskopf, Whitcomb's lack of belief in God allows him to see religion as a useful tool.

The ambitious, foolish, and compulsive Colonel Cathcart dominates the second half of this section, which focuses on the dehumanizing power of bureaucracy. Colonel Cathcart wants to be a general, for no reason other than that he is not a general now. His ludicrous tallying of black eyes and feathers in his cap would be amusing if it did not directly result in his unfailing willingness to risk his men's lives. As it is, Colonel Cathcart is only sickeningly amusing. When Chapter 21 reveals that he does not have a chance of becoming a general, his arbitrary increase of the number of missions his men must fly seems even more meaningless. The poor, ineffectual chaplain wants very much to help Yossarian and his friends, but all his moral convictions are frail and flimsy before the unanswerable authority of men like Cathcart and Korn.

The chaplain's sensation of déjà vu reminds us that in the disordered temporal structure of Heller's story, some events do actually happen twice. But the chaplain defines his déjà vu not in terms of time but as "the subtle, recurring confusion between illusion and reality"—a confusion that becomes quite serious in these chapters.

Yossarian, for example, constructs illusory sicknesses, but doctors are inexplicably unable or unwilling to tell the difference between real and artificial sickness. Frequently, these sicknesses take on the illusory nature of performances. In Chapter 18, Yossarian's admiration for the performance of the man who sees everything twice leads him to imitate that performance. When the man dies in the night, however, Yossarian does not acknowledge the authenticity of the man's sickness; instead, he decides that the man took his performance too far. In order to avoid encountering the ultimate realities of the war—death, pain, and fighting—the men create illusions that blur the lines between what is real and what is not.

CHAPTERS 22–26

SUMMARY — CHAPTER 22: MILO THE MAYOR

The enigmatic references to Snowden's death are finally cleared up; Snowden's death is the moment at which Yossarian loses his nerve. Flying a mission after Colonel Korn's extravagant briefing, Snowden is killed when Dobbs goes crazy and seizes the plane's controls from Huple. As he dies, Snowden pleads for Yossarian's help, saying he is cold. Dobbs is a terrible pilot and a wreck of a man; he later tells Yossarian that he plans to kill Colonel Cathcart before he raises the required number of missions again. Dobbs sees this action as the only way to respond to Cathcart's foolhardiness. When he asks for Yossarian's approval, Yossarian is unable to give it, and Dobbs abandons his plan.

The narrator then describes an episode in which Orr, Yossarian, and Milo take a trip to stock up on supplies. As they travel, Orr and Yossarian gradually realize the extent of Milo's control over the black market and his vast international influence: he is the mayor of Palermo, the assistant governor-general of Malta, the vice-shah of Oran, the caliph of Baghdad, the imam of Damascus, the sheik of Araby, and is worshipped as a god in parts of Africa. Every region has embraced him because he has revitalized their economies with his syndicate, in which everybody has a share. Nevertheless, throughout their trip, Orr and Yossarian are forced to sleep in the plane while Milo enjoys lavish palaces, and they are finally awakened in the middle of the night so that Milo can rush his shipment of red bananas to their next stop.

Summary — Chapter 23: Nately's Old Man

One evening, Nately finds his whore in Rome again after a long search. He tries to convince Yossarian and Aarfy to take two of her friends for thirty dollars each. Aarfy objects, stating that he has never had to pay for sex. Nately's whore is sick of Nately and begins to swear at him. Hungry Joe arrives, and the group abandons Aarfy and goes to the apartment building where the girls live. Here the men find a seemingly endless flow of naked young women, and Hungry Joe is torn between taking in the scene and rushing back for his camera. Nately argues about nationalism and moral duty with an old man who lives in the building: the old man claims Italy is doing better than America in the war because, as Italy has already been occupied, Italians are no longer being killed. He then points out that even America probably won't last as long as frogs, which have been around for five hundred million years. The patriotic, idealistic Nately argues somewhat haltingly for America's international supremacy and the values it represents. But he is troubled by the fact that the old man reminds him of his father. Nately's whore tortures Nately with her indifference, eventually abandoning him and going to bed while he argues with the old man. When Nately finally does get to sleep with his whore the next morning, her little sister almost immediately interrupts them.

Summary — Chapter 24: Milo

By April, Milo's influence is massive: he controls the international black market, plays a major role in the world economy, and uses air force planes from countries all over the world to carry his supply shipments. The planes are repainted with an "M & M Enterprises" logo, but Milo continues to insist that everybody has a share in his syndicate. Milo contracts with the Germans to bomb the Americans and with the Americans to shoot down German planes. German antiaircraft guns contracted by Milo even shot down Mudd, the dead man in Yossarian's tent, for which Yossarian holds a grudge against Milo. Milo wants Yossarian's help to concoct a solution for unloading his massive holdings of Egyptian cotton, which he cannot sell and which threaten to ruin his entire operation. One evening after dinner, Milo's planes begin to bomb Milo's own camp: he has landed another contract with the Germans, and dozens of men are wounded and killed during the attack. Almost everyone wants to end M & M Enterprises right then, but Milo shows them how much money they have all made, and almost all of the survivors forgive him. While Yossarian sits naked in a tree watching Snowden's funeral, Milo seeks him out to talk to him about the cotton. He gives Yossarian some chocolate-covered cotton and tries to convince him it is really candy. Yossarian tells Milo to ask the government to buy his cotton, and Milo is struck by the intelligence of the idea.

Summary — Chapter 25: The Chaplain
The chaplain is troubled that no one seems to treat him as a regular human being and everyone is uncomfortable in his presence. Furthermore, he is intimidated by the soldiers and generally ineffectual as a religious leader. He grows increasingly miserable and is sustained solely by the religious visions he has seen since his arrival, including the vision of the naked man in the tree at Snowden's funeral. (The naked man was, of course, Yossarian.) He dreams of his wife and children dying horribly in his absence. He tries to see Major Major about the number of missions the men are asked to fly but, like everyone else, finds that Major Major will not allow him into his office except when he is out. On the way to see Major Major a second time, the chaplain encounters Flume, Chief White Halfoat's old roommate, who is so afraid of having his throat slit while he sleeps that he has begun living in the forest. The chaplain then learns that Colonel Cathcart has promoted Corporal Whitcomb to sergeant for an idea that the colonel believes will land him in the *Saturday Evening Post*. The chaplain tries to mingle with the men at the officers' club, but Colonel Cathcart periodically throws him out. The chaplain begins doubting everything, even God.

Summary — Chapter 26: Aarfy
The night Nately falls in love with his whore she sits naked from the waist down in a room full of enlisted men playing blackjack. None of the enlisted men is interested except Nately, but she eventually gets sick of him and refuses to accept the money he offers her to stay. Aarfy calls her a slut, and Nately is deeply offended. Aarfy is the navigator of the flight on which Yossarian is finally hit by flak; Yossarian is wounded in the leg and taken to the hospital, where he and Dunbar change identities by ordering lower-ranking men to trade beds with them. Dunbar pretends to be A. Fortiori. Finally, they are caught by Nurse Cramer and Nurse Duckett, who takes Yossarian by the ear and puts him back to bed.

ANALYSIS — CHAPTERS 22–26

The bombing run during which Snowden dies has been alluded to for several chapters, but the details have never been fully explained. The beginning of Chapter 22 provides a few of those details and underlines the narrative importance of the event. The novel's incessant references to the incident have two narrative purposes. First, they emphasize the narrative's circular chronological organization. The event that has so traumatized Yossarian does not recede into the past as Yossarian moves through time; rather, he continually returns to it, unable to escape. Second, the constant references to Snowden's death build up suspense, making the Avignon mission one of the novel's climaxes. Even though this mission occurs chronologically before many other events in the novel, we have to wait until almost the end of the novel to find out exactly what happened on the mission. By telling his story out of chronological order, Heller can place whatever climactic events he wants at the end of the novel, since he is not bound by temporal restraints.

The bombing of Avignon is just one of the many ways in which this section continues to show Yossarian's attempt to hold onto his life and his humanity in the face of the war. The chaplain struggles similarly in this section to remain sane despite his nightmarish life. The chaplain is treated as an outsider by everyone, doubts the moral standards that have governed his life, and endures horrible fantasies of his wife and children dying violent deaths. Just as the idea of the hospital as a place for respectfully coming to terms with death is undermined in the previous section, the idea of the chaplain as a source of spiritual stability and reason in the face of a disorienting and upsetting war is undermined in this section.

Milo Minderbinder is one of the most complex figures in the novel, and the syndicate that he heads is one of its most elusive symbols. On the one hand, the syndicate gives Heller an opportunity to parody the economic activity of large-market capitalism. The extraordinary rationalization by which Milo is able to buy eggs for seven cents apiece and sell them for five cents apiece while still turning a profit is one of the most tortuously sublime moments in the novel, even if it makes only shaky economic sense. Milo claims that at every stage he actually buys and sells the eggs to his own syndicate, thereby somehow retaining the money that he spends to buy the eggs. But, if he buys the eggs with the same resources that he bolsters by selling the eggs, all he is doing is moving money from one place to another. We can easily reduce the bizarre logic that governs Milo's syndicate to nonsense, because we understand the impossibility of Milo's money-making scheme. Yet, though it is completely illogical and unjustifiable, like many concepts in the novel, Milo's syndicate does make money. Whether or not the logic makes sense is irrelevant; the end result defies those who try to explain the process.

The syndicate also represents an almost socialist collectivity—in this enterprise governed by amoral expediency, "everybody has a share." In this light, the syndicate becomes almost a parody of communism as well as capitalism: it is nominally a collective governed by all but is actually run by a single despot. The economic rationalization of the syndicate resembles the moral rationalization of a dehumanized collective, which might agree that it is in everybody's best interest for Milo to bomb his own squadron and kill, wound, and maim a number of his fellow soldiers.

Heller creates a tension between Yossarian's feelings about Milo and our feelings about Milo. Yossarian is undeniably the moral compass of the novel, and he seems to like Milo, which suggests that we too should sympathize with him. But Milo is continually presented as a threatening figure. While Yossarian sits naked in the tree at Snowden's funeral in a highly biblical scene, Milo almost seems like the serpent in the Garden of Eden, there to tempt the innocent with chocolate-covered cotton and the promise of a fast buck.

The absurd proportions of Milo's empire clue us in to an aspect of Catch-22 that, until this section, has been rather subtle: the novel's element of hyperbole. Despite their ridiculous names, all the men in Yossarian's squadron might possibly have lived during WWII. Milo, however, is a completely impossible figure. All along, Heller has created minor absurdities, such as the way the soldier in white has the fluids from his groin directed right back into his IV drip. In this section, he creates a major absurdity in the vastness of Milo's domain, which allows us to know with absolute certainty that Catch-22 is intended more as an allegory than as a realistic portrait of army life.

CHAPTERS 27–31

SUMMARY — CHAPTER 27: NURSE DUCKETT
The next morning, while Nurse Duckett is smoothing the sheets at the foot of his bed, Yossarian thrusts his hand up her skirt. She shrieks and rushes away, and Dunbar grabs her bosom from behind. When a furious doctor finally rescues her, Yossarian tries to plead

insanity—he says that he has a recurring dream about a fish. He is assigned an appointment with Major Sanderson, the hospital psychiatrist. Sanderson, however, is more interested in discussing his own problems than Yossarian's. Yossarian's friends visit him in the hospital, Dobbs again offers to kill Colonel Cathcart, and, finally, after Yossarian admits that he thinks that people are trying to kill him and that he has not adjusted to the war, Major Sanderson decides that Yossarian really is crazy and should be sent home. But, because of the identity mix-up perpetrated by Yossarian and Dunbar earlier in their hospital stay, there is a mistake, and A. Fortiori is sent home instead. Furious, Yossarian goes to see Doc Daneeka, but Doc Daneeka will not ground Yossarian for his insanity, rhetorically asking who would fight if all the crazy men got sent home.

Summary – Chapter 28: Dobbs

Yossarian goes to see Dobbs and tells him to go ahead and kill Colonel Cathcart. But Dobbs has finished his sixty missions and is waiting to be sent home; he no longer has a reason to kill Colonel Cathcart. When Yossarian says that Colonel Cathcart will simply raise the number of missions again, Dobbs says that he will wait and see but that perhaps Orr would help Yossarian kill the colonel. Orr crashed his plane again while Yossarian was in the hospital and was fished out of the ocean—none of the life jackets in his plane worked because Milo took out the carbon dioxide tanks to use for making ice cream sodas. Now, Orr is tinkering with the stove that he is trying to build in his and Yossarian's tent, and he suggests that Yossarian try flying a mission with him for practice in case he ever has to make a crash landing. Yossarian broods about the rumored second mission to Bologna. Orr is making noise and irritating him, and Yossarian imagines killing him, which Yossarian finds a relaxing thought. They talk about women—Orr says they do not like Yossarian, and Yossarian replies that they are crazy. Orr tells Yossarian that he knows Yossarian has asked not to fly with him, and he offers to tell Yossarian why a naked girl was hitting him with her shoe outside Nately's whore's little sister's room in Rome. Yossarian laughingly declines. The next time Orr flies a mission, he again crashes his plane into the ocean. This time, his survival raft drifts away from the others and he disappears.

Summary — Chapter 29: Peckem

The men are dismayed when they learn that General Peckem has transferred Scheisskopf, now a colonel, to his staff. Peckem is pleased because he thinks the move will increase his strength compared to that of his rival, General Dreedle. Colonel Scheisskopf is dismayed by the news that he cannot bring his wife along and that he will no longer be able to conduct parades every afternoon. Scheisskopf immediately irritates his colleagues in Group Headquarters, and Peckem takes him along for an inspection of Colonel Cathcart's squadron briefing. At the preliminary briefing, the men are displeased to learn that they will be bombing an undefended village into rubble; they don't know that the only purpose of the missions is to impress General Peckem with the clean aerial photography enabled by their bomb patterns. When Peckem and Scheisskopf arrive, Cathcart becomes angry that another colonel has appeared to rival him. He gives the briefing himself, and, though he feels shaky and lacks confidence, he makes it through and congratulates himself on a job well done under pressure.

SUMMARY — CHAPTER 30: DUNBAR
On the bombing run, Yossarian has a flashback to the mission during which Snowden died, and he panics. When McWatt starts pulling daredevil stunts, he threatens to kill McWatt if he does not follow orders. He is worried that McWatt will hold a grudge, but, after the mission, McWatt seems concerned only about Yossarian's health. Yossarian has begun seeing Nurse Duckett, and he enjoys making love to her on the beach. Sometimes, while they sit looking at the ocean, Yossarian thinks about all the people who have died underwater, including Orr and Clevinger. One day, McWatt is buzzing the beach in his plane as a joke, when he accidentally flies too low and the propeller slices Kid Sampson in half. Kid Sampson's body splatters all over the beach. Back at the base, everyone is occupied with the disaster; McWatt, meanwhile, does not land his plane but keeps flying higher and higher. Yossarian runs down the runway yelling at McWatt to come down, but he knows what McWatt is going to do. McWatt crashes his plane into the side of a mountain, killing himself. Colonel Cathcart is so upset that he raises the number of missions to sixty-five.

SUMMARY — CHAPTER 31: MRS. DANEEKA
When Colonel Cathcart learns that Doc Daneeka was also killed in the crash, he raises the number of missions to seventy. Actually, Doc Daneeka was not killed in the crash, but the records—which Doc Daneeka, hating to fly, bribed Yossarian to alter—maintain that the doctor was in the plane with McWatt, collecting some flight

time. Doc Daneeka is surprised to hear that he is dead, and his wife in America, who receives a letter to that effect from the military, is shattered. Heroically, she is cheered to learn that she will be receiving a number of monthly payments from various military departments for the rest of her life, as well as sizable life insurance payments from her husband's insurance company. Husbands of her friends begin to flirt with her, and she dyes her hair.

In Pianosa, Doc Daneeka is ostracized by the men, who blame him for the increased number of missions they are required to fly. He is no longer allowed to practice medicine and realizes that, in one sense, he really is dead. He sends a passionate letter to his wife begging her to alert the authorities that he is still alive. She considers the possibility, but after receiving a form letter from Colonel Cathcart expressing regret over her husband's death, she moves her children to Lansing, Michigan, and leaves no forwarding address.

ANALYSIS — CHAPTERS 27–31

This section works through an increasingly macabre surrealism that climaxes with the manslaughter of Kid Sampson and suicide of McWatt. The strange psychological examinations and identity games in the hospital provide Heller with the opportunity to parody modern psychotherapy, which he does with scathing cleverness—Major Sanderson's insistence on discussing his own late puberty is one of the funniest characterizations in the novel. It also lends some weight to the idea of insanity that circulates throughout the novel; the men are always accusing each other of being crazy, and Yossarian even finds insanity a desirable trait, because it will get him out of the war—or would, if not for Catch-22.

Although the novel does not seem to follow a chronological pattern—being composed primarily of episodes that are memories, flashbacks, or character descriptions and having very little grasp on what exactly the current moment is—the climax of these three chapters demonstrates that the novel as a whole still has a somewhat conventional narrative shape. That is, the memories and flashbacks that make up the first two-thirds of the novel lead up to the fatigue and frustration with war that form the background for the events in these chapters. The war transitions from a surreal series of events whose absurdity can be lightly parodied to a reality that is a serious and heavy weight on Yossarian and his squadron. Furthermore, the events in these chapters—particularly the two deaths—shift the narrative from the brilliant parody of the preceding sections into an extremely dark humor that borders on seriousness. The increasing strain the war is placing on Yossarian's psyche is evident in the scene in which he contemplates murdering Orr and finds the idea a relaxing one; it is this thought alone that allows him to tolerate his roommate's prattling.

Orr's disappearance and presumed death come as something of a shock. In fact, one of the most remarkable aspects of *Catch-22* is the way that Heller manages to catch us off guard each time one of Yossarian's friends dies. In part, this aspect is a virtue of the novel's chronology—with so much jumping forward and backward in time, it becomes easy to think of the lives of the characters as existing in a sort of vacuum, without beginning or end. Of course, such is not the case, and the men's deaths are sharp reminders that even in the novel time moves forward and people are fragile. Yossarian is not in need of such a reminder: he is haunted by the death of Snowden and reaches a moment of murderous rage toward McWatt shortly after flashing back to Snowden's death. Yossarian's fierce desire to live makes him seem heroic even in his moments of cowardice. As he strangles McWatt and yells at him to pull up, it seems only just for McWatt to obey.

The absurd chapter on the death of Doc Daneeka represents perhaps the most extreme moment of bureaucratic confusion in the entire novel. Paperwork has the power to make a living man officially dead, and the bureaucracy would rather lose the man than try to confront the forms. Painfully, Mrs. Daneeka becomes complicit in her husband's red-tape murder when she decides to take the insurance payments as a higher authority than his own letter protesting that he is really alive. Doc Daneeka thus realizes that he is essentially dead and that death is a matter of paperwork rather than biology. The soldiers' powerlessness over their own lives extends even to their own deaths, which can be forced upon them not only by the shooting of a gun but also by the fall of a stamp.

CHAPTERS 32–37

SUMMARY — CHAPTER 32: YO-YO'S ROOMIES
The cold weather comes, and Kid Sampson's legs remain on the beach, since no one will retrieve them. The first things Yossarian remembers when he wakes up each morning are Kid Sampson's legs and Snowden. When Orr never returns, four new roommates, a group of shiny-faced twenty-one-year-olds who have never seen combat, join Yossarian. They clown around, calling him "Yo-Yo,"

rousing in him a murderous hatred. Yossarian tries to persuade Chief White Halfoat to move in with them and scare the new officers away, but Halfoat has decided to move into the hospital to die of pneumonia. Yossarian begins to feel more protective toward the men, but they then burn Orr's birch logs and suddenly move Mudd's belongings out of the tent—the dead man who has lived there for so long is abruptly gone. Yossarian panics and flees to Rome with Hungry Joe the day before Nately's whore enjoys a good night's sleep and wakes the next morning to discover that she is in love.

SUMMARY — CHAPTER 33: NATELY'S WHORE
In Rome, Yossarian misses Nurse Duckett and goes searching in vain for Luciana. He accompanies Nately on a mission to rescue his whore from some army officers who will not let her leave their hotel room. After the rescue and a good night's sleep, Nately's whore falls deeply in love with Nately, and they languish in bed together until her little sister dives in with them. Nately begins to have wild fantasies of moving his whore and her sister back to America and bringing the sister up like his own child, but when his whore hears that he no longer wants her to go out hustling, she becomes furious and an argument ensues. The other men try to intervene, and Nately tries to convince them that they can all move to the same suburb and work for his father. He tries to forbid his whore from ever speaking again to the old man in the whore's hotel, and she becomes even angrier. But she still misses Nately when he leaves, and she is furious with Yossarian when he punches Nately in the face and breaks his nose.

SUMMARY — CHAPTER 34: THANKSGIVING
Yossarian breaks Nately's nose on Thanksgiving after Milo gets all the men drunk on bottles of cheap whiskey. Yossarian goes to bed early but wakes up to the sound of machine-gun fire. At first he is terrified, but he quickly realizes that a group of men are firing machine guns as a prank. Furious, he takes his gun to exact revenge. Nately tries to stop him, and Yossarian breaks his nose. Nately is in the hospital the next morning, and Yossarian feels terribly guilty for having broken his nose. They encounter the chaplain in the hospital. He has lied in order to be admitted, claiming to have a disease called Wisconsin shingles. He can now feel wonderful since he has learned how to rationalize vice into virtue. Suddenly, the soldier in white is wheeled into the room, and Dunbar panics. Dunbar begins screaming, and soon everyone in the ward begins screaming as well. Nurse Duckett warns Yossarian that she overheard some doctors talking

about how they planned to "disappear" Dunbar. Yossarian goes to warn his friend but cannot find him.

SUMMARY — CHAPTER 35: MILO THE MILITANT

When Chief White Halfoat finally dies of pneumonia and Nately finishes his seventy missions, Yossarian begs Nately not to volunteer to fly more than seventy missions. But Nately does not want to be sent home until he can take his whore with him. Yossarian asks for help from Milo, who immediately goes to see Colonel Cathcart about having himself assigned to more combat missions. Milo has finally been exposed as the tyrannical fraud he is. He has no intention of giving anyone a real share of the syndicate, but his power and influence are at their peak and everyone admires him. He pretends to feel guilty for not doing his duty—flying missions—and connivingly asks the deferential Colonel Cathcart to assign him to more dangerous combat duties. Milo tells Colonel Cathcart that someone else will have to run the syndicate, and Colonel Cathcart volunteers himself and Colonel Korn. When Milo explains the complex operations of the business to Cathcart, the colonel, falling into Milo's logical traps, declares Milo the only man who could possibly run it and forbids Milo from flying another combat mission. He suggests that he might make the other men fly Milo's missions for him, and if one of those men wins a medal, Milo will get the medal. To make his plan possible, he says, he will ratchet the number of required missions up to eighty. The next morning, the alarm sounds, and the men fly off on a mission that turns out to be particularly deadly. Twelve men are killed, including Dobbs and Nately.

SUMMARY — CHAPTER 36: THE CELLAR

The chaplain is devastated by Nately's death, which he learns about at the airfield where the men are returning from their mission. Suddenly, the chaplain is dragged away by a group of military police who accuse him of an unspecified crime. A colonel accuses the chaplain of forgery and interrogates him. His only evidence is a letter that Yossarian forged in the hospital and signed with the chaplain's name some time ago. He then accuses the chaplain of stealing the plum tomato from Colonel Cathcart and of being Washington Irving. The men in the room idiotically find him guilty of unspecified crimes they assume he has committed and then order him to go about his business while they think of a way to punish him. The chaplain leaves and furiously goes to confront Colonel Korn about the number of missions the men are required to fly. He tells Colonel

Korn that he plans to bring the matter directly to General Dreedle's attention, but the colonel replies gleefully that General Peckem has replaced General Dreedle as wing commander. He then tells the chaplain that he and Colonel Cathcart can make the men fly as many missions as they want to make them fly—they have even transferred Dr. Stubbs, who had offered to ground any man with more than seventy missions, to the Pacific.

SUMMARY — CHAPTER 37: GENERAL SCHEISSKOPF
General Peckem's victory sours quickly. On his first day in charge of General Dreedle's old operation, he learns that Scheisskopf has been promoted to lieutenant general and is now the commanding officer for all combat operations. He is in charge of General Peckem and his entire group, and he intends to make every single man present march in parades.

ANALYSIS — CHAPTERS 32–37
The first part of this section, with Yossarian's young roommates and the story of Nately's whore, returns to the high comedy of the earlier parts of the novel, but with the important difference that Yossarian is on the edge of a breakdown and seems to know it. Orr's disappearance is a very hard blow, and Yossarian is now plagued by thoughts of death and dismemberment. The high comedy comes to an abrupt and unexpected halt with the eerie return of the soldier in white, which is followed immediately by Dunbar's unexplained disappearance and the deaths of Chief White Halfoat, Nately, and Dobbs. The squadron is beginning to fall apart, and even the military bureaucracy is being turned on its thick head by the sudden ousting of General Dreedle in favor of General Peckem, who immediately learns that General Scheisskopf is now his superior officer. Furthermore, Scheisskopf's intention for everyone under his command to march in parades is a ludicrous juxtaposition of irrelevant discipline-building exercises with the realities of war.

As Yossarian's story moves toward its climax, the sense of unknown danger approaching from all sides intensifies markedly, from gunfire in the dark to the disappearance of Dobbs to the chaplain's sudden, disconcerting interrogation for an unspecified crime. (This scene is reminiscent of the scene in Franz Kafka's *The Trial*, in which the novel's protagonist wakes one morning to find himself accused of a crime whose nature no one will describe to him.) The illogical nature of the chaplain's interrogation makes it so terrifying.

If he were accused of a specific crime, or if his interrogators were willing to listen to a word he said, the chaplain would have at least some power over his situation. As it is, all his attempts to clear his name are met with the same illogical arguments, and he can do absolutely nothing; he realizes that his captors could beat him to death if they wanted to and he couldn't stop them. The chaplain's plight is similar to that of all the men in the squadron: their lives are in the hands of others, and their logical desire to go free because they are innocent is meaningless in a world without logic.

Another highly restrictive force surrounding the squadron is the fact that no goal seems to be achievable. As soon as the men complete their missions, the required number is raised; as soon as Orr finishes building his stove, he is shot down and disappears; as soon as Nately's whore falls in love with him, he is killed in combat. It seems almost miraculous that the men have it in them to try to accomplish anything, let alone the thankless task of bombing enemies they have never seen, when almost any action taken to alter the status quo has very negative consequences. However, Heller always stops just short of criticizing the war itself—it would be difficult to argue that fighting Hitler is wrong. Instead, he criticizes the *way* in which the war is carried out.

This section is also one of the only long sequences of chapters told in straight linear time—the same timeline, in fact, that leads right to the end of the novel. Heller uses this long chronological sequence to enhance the sense of momentum building toward a climax. The orderly progression of time corresponds to an increasing disorder in Yossarian's world: the helplessness and lack of control that the men feel spirals to a fever pitch. As things fall apart all around Yossarian, the novel takes on the feel of a moving walkway, leading inexorably toward an unspecified, ominous ending.

Chapters 38–42

Summary — Chapter 38: Kid Sister

Yossarian marches around backward so that no one can sneak up behind him, and he refuses to fly in any more combat missions. When informed of Yossarian's defiance, Colonel Cathcart and Colonel Korn decide to take pity on Yossarian for the death of his friend Nately and send him to Rome to rest. In Rome, he breaks the news of Nately's death to Nately's whore, who tries to kill him with a potato peeler for bringing her the bad news. Her kid sister materializes and also tries to stab him. Covered with stab wounds, Yossarian goes to a Red Cross building to get cleaned up. When he emerges, Nately's whore is waiting in ambush and tries to stab him again. She follows him everywhere, even back to Pianosa, but he retaliates by flying her to a distant location and dropping her in a parachute from the plane. Yossarian still walks around backward, and, as word spreads that he has refused to fly more combat missions, men begin to approach him at night to ask him if it is true and to tell him that they hope he gets away with it. Worried, Yossarian's superior officers offer to assign him only nondangerous missions if he agrees to fly; he refuses, because that would mean that other men would have to fly his share of dangerous missions. One day, Captain Black tells him that Nately's whore and her kid sister have been flushed out of their apartment by the military police (M.P.'s), and Yossarian is suddenly worried about them.

SUMMARY — CHAPTER 39: THE ETERNAL CITY
Yossarian travels to Rome with Milo, who is disappointed in him for refusing to fly more combat missions. Rome has been bombed and lies in ruins, and the apartment complex where the whores lived is a deserted shambles. Yossarian finds the old woman who lived in the complex sobbing. She tells Yossarian that the only right the soldiers had to chase the girls away was the right of Catch-22, which says "they have a right to do anything we can't stop them from doing." Yossarian asks if they had Catch-22 written down and if they showed it to her, and she says that Catch-22 stipulates that they don't have to show her Catch-22. Yossarian knows that Catch-22 does not exist but that its nonexistence does not matter, because everyone believes that it exists. Milo agrees to help Yossarian track down the kid sister, but he becomes distracted when he learns about huge profits to be made in trafficking illegal tobacco. He slinks away, and Yossarian is left to wander the dark streets through a horrible night filled with grotesqueries and loathsome sights: men beat dogs and children, a soldier convulses helplessly, a woman is raped, and the sidewalk is strewn with broken human teeth. He returns to his apartment late in the night to find that Aarfy has raped and killed a maid. The M.P.'s burst in. They apologize to Aarfy for intruding and arrest Yossarian for being in Rome without a pass.

SUMMARY — CHAPTER 40: CATCH-22
Back at Pianosa, Colonel Cathcart and Colonel Korn want to send Yossarian home, but Catch-22 prevents them. They offer

Yossarian a deal: they will ground him and send him home if he will agree to like them. He will be promoted to major and all he will have to do is support the two colonels. Yossarian realizes that the deal is a frankly atrocious betrayal of the men in his squadron, who will still have to fly the eighty missions, but he persuades himself to take the deal anyway. The prospect of going home fills him with joy. As Yossarian departs from Colonel Cathcart's office, Nately's whore appears, disguised as a private, and stabs him until he falls unconscious.

SUMMARY — CHAPTER 41: SNOWDEN

Man was matter, that was Snowden's secret.... Bury
him and he'll rot, like other kinds of garbage....
Ripeness was all.

(See QUOTATIONS, *p. 55)*

In the hospital, a group of doctors argues over Yossarian while the fat, angry colonel who interrogated the chaplain interrogates him. Finally, the doctors knock him out and operate on him. When he wakes, he dimly perceives visits from Aarfy and the chaplain. He tells the chaplain about his deal with Cathcart and Korn, and then assures him that he isn't going to do it. He vaguely remembers a malignant, almost supernatural man jeering at him, "We've got your pal," shortly after his operation. He then tells the chaplain that his "pal" must have been one of his friends who was killed in the war. He realizes that his only friend still living is Hungry Joe, but then the chaplain tells him that Hungry Joe has died—in his sleep, with Huple's cat on his face.

Later, Yossarian wakes up to find a mean-looking man in a hospital gown leering at him, saying, "We've got your pal." He asks who his pal is, and the man tells Yossarian he will find out. Yossarian lunges for him, but the man glides away and vanishes. Yossarian then has a flashback to Snowden's death, which he relives in all its agony. Smiling at him wanly, Snowden whimpers, "I'm cold." Yossarian reassures him and tries to mend the wound in Snowden's leg, thinking that he will live. Finally, Yossarian opens up Snowden's flak suit, and Snowden's insides spill out all over him. Yossarian remembers the secret he read in those entrails: "The spirit gone, man is garbage." He thinks to himself that man is matter and that, without the spirit, man will rot like garbage.

SUMMARY & ANALYSIS

SUMMARY — CHAPTER 42: YOSSARIAN

In the hospital, Yossarian tries to explain to Major Danby why he can no longer go through with Cathcart and Korn's deal: he won't sell himself so short, and he won't betray the memory of his dead friends. Yossarian tells Danby that he plans to run away, but Danby tells him that there is no hope, and Yossarian agrees. Suddenly, the chaplain bursts in with the news that Orr has washed ashore in Sweden. Yossarian realizes that Orr must have planned his escape all along and joyfully decides that there is hope after all. He has the chaplain retrieve his clothes and decides to desert the army and run to Sweden, where he can save himself from the madness of the war. As he steps outside, Nately's whore tries to stab him again, and he runs into the distance.

ANALYSIS — CHAPTERS 38–42

This section plunges Yossarian into the deepest, most surreal darkness in the novel—the night in Rome after the disappearance of Nately's whore and her sister is the most wrenching, despairing scene in *Catch-22*—as Yossarian encounters example after example of abuse, neglect, and oppression. This scene culminates in Aarfy's rape and murder of the maid, which finally explodes the question of moral absolutes in war: Yossarian, outraged, repeats the most inviolable of those absolutes—one cannot kill another person—and is then arrested for the meaningless crime of being in Rome without a pass, while Aarfy receives an apology from the police. Obviously, war carries a requirement to kill other people, and, as the old woman who notes the dominance of Catch-22 is aware, this fact undermines every other natural and moral law.

Snowden's death has been hinted at throughout the novel, but it is only in the second-to-last chapter that we are finally allowed to see the scene from beginning to end. Because it is placed near the end of the novel and is so clearly an important event, Snowden's death functions as the technical climax of *Catch-22*, even though it took place before many of the novel's other events. The progression of the scene of Snowden's death is similar to Yossarian's progression throughout the novel: at first, Yossarian thinks that he has control over death and that he can stop Snowden's leg wound from bleeding and save Snowden's life; later, he finds that death is a force utterly outside his control. The "secret" revealed to him here is that man is made of inanimate matter and that no human hands can restore life to a body once it has been destroyed by flak, disease, or drowning.

Yossarian has taken Snowden's secret to heart, and he realizes that the impulse to live is the most important human quality. But the impulse to live is not simply a desire to survive at any cost: Yossarian cannot live as a hypocrite or as a slave; as a result, he decides to incur enormous personal danger by attempting to escape from the military rather than take the safe deal that would betray his friends. Yossarian chooses simply to take his life back into his own hands, openly rejecting (rather than, as the deal would have required, falsely embracing) the mentality of Catch-22 and making his run for freedom. He is inspired in this decision by the rather absurd example of Orr, who has escaped to Sweden.

The appearance of Nately's whore in this section works as a bizarre kind of moral point of reference. Though Yossarian is not responsible for Nately's death, Nately's whore still seems to blame Yossarian, and, to an extent, Yossarian blames himself—at least enough to feel responsible for the whore and her sister. But as long as he refuses to comply with the military authorities, he manages to escape Nately's whore's attempts to murder him. Only when he agrees to the deal with Cathcart and Korn does she succeed in stabbing and seriously injuring him, suggesting that the act of agreeing with these bureaucrats constitutes the metaphorical death of Yossarian. At the end of the novel, when Yossarian makes his escape, the whore's presence is a surprisingly welcome one—and Yossarian succeeds in getting away from her—proof that he is doing the right thing in refusing to sell himself out to the bureaucracy.

IMPORTANT QUOTATIONS EXPLAINED

1.   There was only one catch and that was Catch-22, which specified that a concern for one's own safety in the face of dangers that were real and immediate was the process of a rational mind. Orr was crazy and could be grounded. All he had to do was ask; and as soon as he did, he would no longer be crazy and would have to fly more missions. Orr would be crazy to fly more missions and sane if he didn't, but if he was sane he would have to fly them. If he flew them he was crazy and didn't have to; but if he didn't want to he was sane and had to. Yossarian was moved very deeply by the absolute simplicity of this clause of Catch-22 and let out a respectful whistle. "That's some catch, that Catch-22," he observed. "It's the best there is," Doc Daneeka agreed.

This passage from Chapter 5 marks the novel's first mention of the paradoxical law called "Catch-22." Over the course of the novel, Catch-22 is described in a number of different ways that can be applied to a number of different aspects of wartime life; here, however, Catch-22 affects Yossarian most specifically. Catch-22 is alarmingly persuasive; even Yossarian accepts what seems to be its logical infallibility. But Catch-22 is an abstract thing; we find out later that Yossarian believes that Catch-22 does not really exist. It is a trap made up of words, and words are faulty things, often misrepresenting reality. What is so upsetting about the way Catch-22 is applied throughout the novel is that real men are sent into real peril based on a few unreal and unreliable words.

2.   These three men who hated [Clevinger] spoke his language and wore his uniform, but he saw their loveless faces set immutably into cramped, mean lines of hostility and understood instantly that nowhere in the world, not in all the fascist tanks or planes or submarines, not in the bunker behind the machine guns or mortars or behind the blowing flame throwers, not even among all the expert gunners of the crack Hermann Goering Antiaircraft Division or among the

grisly connivers in all the beer halls in Munich and
everywhere else, were there men who hated him more.

In this passage from Chapter 8, Clevinger has just faced a hearing in
which Lieutenant Scheisskopf and two other officers convict him of
an infraction that he did not commit and sentence him to punishment duty. Their hatred of him forces him to come to terms with one
of the central ironies of Catch-22: the force that drives men from
opposing armies to shoot at and kill each other has nothing to do
with personal hatred. It seems strange to Clevinger that men who
want to kill him do not hate him, whereas men who are ostensibly
his allies hate him deeply.

3.   One of the things [Yossarian] wanted to start screaming
      about was the surgeon's knife that was almost certain to be
      waiting for him and everyone else who lived long enough to
      die. He wondered often how he would ever recognize the
      first chill, flush, twinge, ache, belch, sneeze, stain, lethargy,
      vocal slip, loss of balance or lapse of memory that would
      signal the inevitable beginning of the inevitable end.

This quote from Chapter 17 demonstrates that the war, in confront-
ing Yossarian daily with the possibility of his own death, has not
hardened him to fear; instead, it has made him much more aware of
the value and fragility of life. He cannot stop thinking about all the
ways in which he could possibly die—in addition to antiaircraft fire,
there are plenty of diseases that could kill him. In this passage, Yossarian also dwells on the inevitability of death. He feels trapped in
the army; Catch-22 prevents him from escaping it. But the fact that
he must someday die is an even greater and more inescapable trap,
for even if he manages to wiggle out of the prison of the army, he will
still have to face his death eventually.

QUOTATIONS

4.   "Haven't you got anything humorous that stays away from
waters and valleys and God? I'd like to keep away from the
subject of religion altogether if we can."
        The chaplain was apologetic. "I'm sorry, sir, but I'm
afraid all the prayers I know *are* rather somber in tone and
make at least some passing reference to God."
        "Then let's get some new ones."

In this conversation in Chapter 19, Colonel Cathcart and the chaplain discuss the possibility of saying a group prayer before each mission. Cathcart wants to start saying the prayers because he thinks it
will get him mentioned in the *Saturday Evening Post*; later, he abandons this idea when he hears that the enlisted men will have to be
included along with the officers. By asking to exclude religion from
the prayers, Cathcart shows that he is interested in religion only as a
tool for his own advancement. Actual faith in God has nothing to do
with the chaplain's purpose—at least as far as Cathcart is concerned. Throughout *Catch-22*, the chaplain struggles to maintain
his faith, and he is confronted again and again by men who want to
use religion as a tool without understanding the value of real faith.

5.   Yossarian was cold, too, and shivering uncontrollably. He
felt goose pimples clacking all over him as he gazed down
despondently at the grim secret Snowden had spilled all over
the messy floor. It was easy to read the message in his
entrails. Man was matter, that was Snowden's secret. Drop
him out a window and he'll fall. Set fire to him and he'll
burn. Bury him and he'll rot, like other kinds of garbage.
That was Snowden's secret. Ripeness was all.

This passage occurs in Chapter 41 during the final description of
Snowden's death, in which Snowden's entrails spill out of his stom-
ach and onto the floor. Snowden's death causes Yossarian to realize
that, without the spirit, man is nothing but matter. Yossarian feels
cold, which allows him to identify with Snowden; in Snowden's
entrails, Yossarian can see the prediction of his own death. The final
sentence of this passage, "Ripeness is all," contains a small message
of hope, implying that man can, for a brief period, be truly alive. It
is this kind of ripeness that Yossarian clings to by trying to keep himself alive and, eventually, by deserting the army.

KEY FACTS

FULL TITLE
Catch-22

AUTHOR
Joseph Heller

TYPE OF WORK
Novel

GENRE
War novel; satire

LANGUAGE
English

TIME AND PLACE WRITTEN
1955–1961, New York

DATE OF FIRST PUBLICATION
1961

PUBLISHER
Simon & Schuster, Inc.

NARRATOR
The anonymous narrator is omniscient, seeing and knowing all things. The narrator presents characters and events in a humorous, satirical light but seems to have real sympathy for some of them as well.

POINT OF VIEW
The narrator speaks in the third person, focusing mostly on what Yossarian does and what Yossarian thinks and feels. Occasionally, the narrator also shows us how other characters, such as the chaplain or Hungry Joe, experience the world around them.

TONE
The narrator presents ridiculous behavior and illogical arguments in a flatly satirical tone, never stating outright that matters are funny, but always making the reader aware of how outrageously bizarre the characters and situations are.

TENSE

The story is written in the past tense. Although the book settles into a more chronological order as it approaches its end, most of *Catch-22* is told out of sequence, with events from the past mixed in with events from the present.

SETTING (TIME)

Near the end of World War II

SETTING (PLACE)

Pianosa, a small island off the coast of Italy. Although Pianosa is a real place, Heller has taken some creative liberties with it, enlarging it to hold all the action of the novel.

PROTAGONIST

John Yossarian, an Air Force captain and bombardier stationed in Pianosa

MAJOR CONFLICT

Yossarian struggles to stay alive, despite the many parties who seem to want him dead.

RISING ACTION

The rising action in the novel's present time is Yossarian's growing certainty that he will never be allowed to go home. Alongside Yossarian's certainty is a second subplot that takes place in the past: the bombing run on which Snowden was killed. As the novel moves along, we are allowed to see more and more of this pivotal scene.

CLIMAX

The two climaxes of *Catch-22* happen simultaneously. The first climax occurs when Yossarian is offered a choice: he can either face a court-martial or be sent home if he agrees to support Cathcart and Korn. The second climax, which occurs as Yossarian makes his decision, is the final flashback to Snowden's death, in which all the details of this critical event are at last revealed.

FALLING ACTION

Remembering the lesson of Snowden's death, Yossarian decides that he cannot betray the other men in his squadron by forcing them to fly his missions for him. Instead, he decides to desert the army and flee the camp.

THEMES

The absolute power of bureaucracy; loss of religious faith; the impotence of language; the inevitability of death

MOTIFS

Catch-22; number of missions; Washington Irving

SYMBOLS

Chocolate-covered cotton; the soldier in white; aerial photographs

FORESHADOWING

Snowden's death is heavily foreshadowed, but in the unusual vehicle of Yossarian's memories. Yossarian recalls the death very briefly several times near the beginning of *Catch-22*. It is not until the second-to-last chapter that the death is finally described in full.

KEY FACTS

STUDY QUESTIONS & ESSAY TOPICS

STUDY QUESTIONS

1. *Throughout the novel, the idea of Catch-22 is explained in a number of ways. What are some of them? Do any of them represent the real Catch-22, or are they all simply examples of a larger abstract idea? If Catch-22 is an abstract concept, which explanation comes closest to it?*

For most of the novel, Catch-22 defines the maddening, paradoxical thought processes by which the military runs its soldiers' lives; any time Yossarian spies a potential way out of the war, there is a catch, and it is always called Catch-22. Doc Daneeka offers the first explanation: requests to go home are only honored for the insane, but anyone who would ask to be taken off combat duty must necessarily be sane. Another example is Captain Black's Glorious Loyalty Oath Crusade: men are required to sign loyalty oaths before they can eat, but they are not forced to sign loyalty oaths because they are always free to not eat. The officials reason that Major Major must be a communist because he has not signed a loyalty oath, but he is not allowed to sign a loyalty oath because Captain Black won't let him.

This kind of thinking enables the war, and it permeates the novel, even in settings outside the official grasp of Catch-22. Luciana, for instance, will not marry Yossarian because he is crazy, and she knows he is crazy because he wants to marry her. If he did not want to marry her, he would not be crazy, and then she could marry him. The most penetrating explanation of Catch-22 is also the last that the novel offers—when the old woman outside the whorehouse in Rome says that Catch-22 indicates that "they have a right to do anything we can't stop them from doing." She says that Catch-22 is fundamentally inscrutable: the law says that those in power do not have to show Catch-22 to anyone, and the law that says so is Catch-22. This statement confirms what Yossarian has always known: Catch-22 does not really exist; it is merely a justification for the strong to use against the weak. It is the abstract mechanism at the heart of

Catch-22, the mechanism by which the military can force human beings with the desire to live into endlessly dehumanizing situations in which they are likely to be killed. The unanswerable paradox of unearned power means that those in power can do anything that the subjects of that power cannot stop them from doing.

2.   *Discuss Milo. Does the fact that he seems to exist outside military authority make him a positive figure or a negative one?*

In one sense, Milo is a crusader against the arbitrary regulations of the military bureaucracy. He ignores the army's regulations and borrows both planes and supplies in order to increase his profits. Unlike many of the men, who feel powerless in the face of the authorities, Milo exists completely outside the bureaucracy and seems to get away with it.

But, while Milo certainly represents an individual's triumph in the face of a dehumanizing organization, he also lacks morals and consideration for others. He is a perfect symbol of what is wrong with free-market capitalism: it encourages men to profit from the losses of others. A minor example of Milo's selfishness is the way he makes Yossarian and Orr sleep in the plane while he himself sleeps in luxurious palaces; a major example is the way he claims that "everyone has a share" in his syndicate, only to keep all the profits for himself. By the end of the novel, Milo is selling chocolate-covered cotton—a product more meaningless than anything the army's bureaucracy could dream up. In a sense, as he has gained power, Milo has become like the authoritarian forces he defies, sacrificing real value for personal gain.

3.   *What role do women play in Catch-22?*

Because all of the enlistees in Yossarian's squadron are male, women play only a minor role in the novel. They act as barometers by which we can measure the qualities of the men who interact with them. Yossarian, for example, falls passionately in love with every woman he meets—a symptom of his desperate desire to seize as much of life as possible before he dies. One example of this desire occurs at the Avignon briefing, where Yossarian starts an epidemic of moaning because he realizes that he will never get the chance to sleep with General Dreedle's beautiful assistant.

Women are also markers of the deep immorality and tragedy of war. Luciana, very beautiful and earnest, is deeply ashamed of a scar on her back that she got during an air raid. Nately's whore has been forced by the war to go into prostitution; she is utterly indifferent to everything until she falls in love with Nately, and he is killed almost immediately afterward. She then seeks revenge on Yossarian, who brings her the bad news about Nately, and keeps trying to stab him. She acts as proof that evil is not without consequence and that the pain that war inflicts on the world will not simply disappear.

SUGGESTED ESSAY TOPICS

1. *Think about chronology in the novel. How does the disordered, tangential presentation of events affect the flow of the story? What devices does Heller employ to allow the reader to piece together the order of events? What kind of unified narrative, if any, ultimately emerges? What does this portrayal say about the idea of time in Catch-22?*

2. *Discuss the chaplain. How does his religious faith develop and change as the story progresses? What does his timidity say about the power of moral absolutes in the world of the military? What is the significance of his sensation of déjà vu?*

3. *Think about the novel's use of setting and scene. What effect do the rapid shifts between the base and the hospital, or between Pianosa and Rome, have on the presentation of the story? What does each location seem to represent?*

4. *What does Snowden's death mean to Yossarian?*

5. *How does Catch-22 differ from other war stories?*

REVIEW & RESOURCES

QUIZ

1. What is the name of the nurse with whom Yossarian sleeps?

    A. Nurse Dreedle
    B. Nurse Cramer
    C. Nurse White
    D. Nurse Duckett

2. What happens on the mission for which Yossarian receives a medal?

    A. He shoots down an enemy plane
    B. He forces his entire squadron to retreat
    C. His plane stalls as he circles
    D. A younger pilot is killed by shrapnel

3. What is the name of the dead man in Yossarian's tent?

    A. Bones
    B. Black
    C. Cadwallader
    D. Mudd

4. To which country does Yossarian decide to desert?

    A. Sweden
    B. Syria
    C. The U.S.A.
    D. Spain

5. For what publication was Hungry Joe a photographer before the war?

    A. *The Herald-Tribune*
    B. *The Saturday Evening Post*
    C. *Playboy*
    D. *Life*

6. From which publication does Colonel Cathart get the idea of praying before missions?

   A. *The Herald-Tribune*
   B. *The Saturday Evening Post*
   C. *Playboy*
   D. *Life*

7. What did Major Major Major Major's mother intend to name him?

   A. Minor
   B. Jeremy
   C. Caleb
   D. C-Flat

8. When Major Major gets bored of signing Washington Irving's name, what other name does he use?

   A. John Yossarian
   B. John Milton
   C. John Donne
   D. Johnny Appleseed

9. Which member of the squadron is an expert at Ping-Pong?

   A. Yossarian
   B. Orr
   C. Hungry Joe
   D. Appleby

10. What is the name of the man who hides out in the woods because he is afraid of having his throat cut?

    A. Flounce
    B. Flume
    C. Flutter
    D. Fling

11. Which city does the squadron bomb when Yossarian refuses to participate?

    A.   Bologna
    B.   Bresaola
    C.   Liguria
    D.   Bari

12. Why will Luciana and Yossarian not get married?

    A.   She is afraid he will get killed
    B.   Luciana already has a husband
    C.   Luciana thinks Yossarian is crazy
    D.   Yossarian cannot leave his squadron

13. Which of the following does Yossarian see as he wanders through Rome?

    A.   A priest praying in a church
    B.   A dry fountain
    C.   A maid raped and killed by Aarfy
    D.   A man begging for money

14. What is Kid Sampson doing when he gets sliced in half?

    A.   Playing with a buzz saw
    B.   Standing on a raft
    C.   Dodging enemy fire
    D.   Playing volleyball

15. How many people parachute to safety before McWatt crashes his plane into a mountain?

    A.   None
    B.   1
    C.   2
    D.   3

16. Where did Doc Daneeka practice medicine before being drafted?

    A. Hollywood
    B. Colorado Springs
    C. Staten Island
    D. Manhattan, Kansas

17. Who does Yossarian pretend to be in the hospital?

    A. A doctor
    B. A nurse
    C. A high-ranking officer
    D. A dying soldier

18. Which holiday does Yossarian spend in the hospital?

    A. Boxing Day
    B. Thanksgiving
    C. Independence Day
    D. Labor Day

19. What do Yossarian's new roommates do with the dead man's things?

    A. They sell them to Milo
    B. They use them to start a fire
    C. They steal them and hide them in their packs
    D. They throw them outside

20. What does the Texan argue that "decent folk" should receive?

    A. Tax cuts
    B. Free health insurance
    C. Extra rations
    D. Extra votes

REVIEW & RESOURCES

21. What improvement does Orr make to Yossarian's tent just before he disappears?

    A.   He finishes putting in a stove
    B.   He paves the floor with bricks
    C.   He finishes installing a secret liquor cabinet
    D.   He constructs an air-raid shelter

22. Why won't Aarfy pay for any prostitutes?

    A.   He is sending all his money home to his sick wife
    B.   He is afraid of getting diseases
    C.   He is proud of never having to pay for sex
    D.   He has been impotent ever since the Bologna mission

23. Which of Yossarian's friends is still alive at the end of *Catch-22*?

    A.   Nately
    B.   Orr
    C.   Chief White Halfoat
    D.   Dobbs

24. Where does the chaplain live?

    A.   In a nearby church
    B.   In a tent in the forest
    C.   In the barracks with the men
    D.   In the basement beneath the kitchen

25. How does Hungry Joe die?

    A.   He starves to death
    B.   In his sleep
    C.   He drowns on his way back to the U.S.
    D.   Chief White Halfoat cuts his throat

ANSWER KEY:

1: D; 2: D; 3: D; 4: A; 5: D; 6: B; 7: C; 8: B; 9: D; 10: B; 11: A; 12: C;
13: C; 14: B; 15: C; 16: C; 17: D; 18: B; 19: B; 20: D; 21: A; 22: C; 23:
B; 24: B; 25: B

SUGGESTIONS FOR FURTHER READING

BLOOM, HAROLD, ed. *Joseph Heller's* CATCH-22. Philadelphia: Chelsea House Publishers, 2001.

KILEY, FREDERICK T., and WALTER MCDONALD, eds. *A* CATCH-22 *Casebook*. New York: Crowell, 1973.

MERRILL, ROBERT. *Joseph Heller*. Boston: Twayne Publishers, 1987.

NAGEL, JAMES, ed. *Critical Essays on Catch-22*. Encino, California: Dickenson Publishing Co., 1974.

PINSKER, SANFORD. *Understanding Joseph Heller*. Columbia, South Carolina: University of South Carolina Press, 1991.

POTTS, STEPHEN W. CATCH-22: *Antiheroic Antinovel*. Boston: Twayne Publishers, 1989.

WOODSON, JON. *A Study of Joseph Heller's* CATCH-22: *Going Around Twice*. New York: P. Lang, 2001.

SparkNotes™ Literature Guides

1984
The Adventures of Huckleberry Finn
The Adventures of Tom Sawyer
The Aeneid
All Quiet on the Western Front
And Then There Were None
Angela's Ashes
Animal Farm
Anna Karenina
Anne of Green Gables
Anthem
Antony and Cleopatra
Aristotle's Ethics
As I Lay Dying
As You Like It
Atlas Shrugged
The Awakening
The Autobiography of Malcolm X
The Bean Trees
The Bell Jar
Beloved
Beowulf
Billy Budd
Black Boy
Bless Me, Ultima
The Bluest Eye
Brave New World
The Brothers Karamazov
The Call of the Wild
Candide
The Canterbury Tales
Catch-22
The Catcher in the Rye
The Chocolate War
The Chosen
Cold Mountain
Cold Sassy Tree
The Color Purple
The Count of Monte Cristo
Crime and Punishment
The Crucible
Cry, the Beloved Country
Cyrano de Bergerac
David Copperfield

Death of a Salesman
The Death of Socrates
The Diary of a Young Girl
A Doll's House
Don Quixote
Dr. Faustus
Dr. Jekyll and Mr. Hyde
Dracula
Dune
East of Eden
Edith Hamilton's Mythology
Emma
Ethan Frome
Fahrenheit 451
Fallen Angels
A Farewell to Arms
Farewell to Manzanar
Flowers for Algernon
For Whom the Bell Tolls
The Fountainhead
Frankenstein
The Giver
The Glass Menagerie
Gone With the Wind
The Good Earth
The Grapes of Wrath
Great Expectations
The Great Gatsby
Greek Classics
Grendel
Gulliver's Travels
Hamlet
The Handmaid's Tale
Hard Times
Harry Potter and the Sorcerer's Stone
Heart of Darkness
Henry IV, Part I
Henry V
Hiroshima
The Hobbit
The House of Seven Gables
I Know Why the Caged Bird Sings
The Iliad
Inferno
Inherit the Wind
Invisible Man

Jane Eyre
Johnny Tremain
The Joy Luck Club
Julius Caesar
The Jungle
The Killer Angels
King Lear
The Last of the Mohicans
Les Miserables
A Lesson Before Dying
The Little Prince
Little Women
Lord of the Flies
The Lord of the Rings
Macbeth
Madame Bovary
A Man for All Seasons
The Mayor of Casterbridge
The Merchant of Venice
A Midsummer Night's Dream
Moby Dick
Much Ado About Nothing
My Antonia
Narrative of the Life of Frederick Douglass
Native Son
The New Testament
Night
Notes from Underground
The Odyssey
The Oedipus Plays
Of Mice and Men
The Old Man and the Sea
The Old Testament
Oliver Twist
The Once and Future King
One Day in the Life of Ivan Denisovich
One Flew Over the Cuckoo's Nest
One Hundred Years of Solitude
Othello
Our Town
The Outsiders

Paradise Lost
A Passage to India
The Pearl
The Picture of Dorian Gray
Poe's Short Stories
A Portrait of the Artist as a Young Man
Pride and Prejudice
The Prince
A Raisin in the Sun
The Red Badge of Courage
The Republic
Richard III
Robinson Crusoe
Romeo and Juliet
The Scarlet Letter
A Separate Peace
Silas Marner
Sir Gawain and the Green Knight
Slaughterhouse-Five
Snow Falling on Cedars
Song of Solomon
The Sound and the Fury
Steppenwolf
The Stranger
Streetcar Named Desire
The Sun Also Rises
A Tale of Two Cities
The Taming of the Shrew
The Tempest
Tess of the d'Ubervilles
Their Eyes Were Watching God
Things Fall Apart
The Things They Carried
To Kill a Mockingbird
To the Lighthouse
Treasure Island
Twelfth Night
Ulysses
Uncle Tom's Cabin
Walden
War and Peace
Wuthering Heights
A Yellow Raft in Blue Water